# The Augusta Principles

## Timeless Business Lessons from the World's Premier Golf Club

JOHN SABINO

VB
VALUABLE BOOK GROUP

"Augusta, Georgia, has been very good to this club
and to the Masters Tournament, and I look at our
involvement with our community as being a
relationship. It's not a transaction."


-    Fred Ridley, chairman of Augusta National Golf Club

Also by John Sabino

*How to Play the World's Most Exclusive Golf Clubs: A Journey through Pine Valley, Royal Melbourne, Augusta, Muirfield, and More*

*Golf's Iron Horse: The Astonishing, Record-Breaking Life of Ralph Kennedy*

*Incredible Golf Stories: Amazing Tales from the Green* (Contributor)

# CONTENTS

# Introduction

It was like leaving a cave and discovering for the first time that there was sunlight. The beauty of the perfect emerald grass was completely unexpected. I was smitten. I went to my first Masters as the Tiger Woods era was beginning in 1997. Although the focus of the media and the fans was understandably on the talented young golfer who would change golf forever, I came away remembering the grass. And how civilized the environment was. Although I had been toiling away in the depths of Wall Street for a decade and had a good understanding of how businesses operated, it struck me that Augusta National was different. But I didn't understand why.

A seed had unknowingly been planted.

The Masters resonated more with me because the juxtaposition to my own experiences was so stark. I worked in New York City, which is a jumble. And a jungle. An exhilarating jungle that gave me energy, but a jungle nonetheless. The contrast between the two worlds stayed in the back of my mind. The matter was never front of mind because I had two kids at home in diapers and a demanding job. I returned to the Masters whenever I could, and each time my love and curiosity for the tournament grew.

She became my secret love, like one a sailor visits occasionally on faraway shores. She was always waiting for me. And each time she looked better.

I'm what you'd call a late bloomer. I didn't excel at sports when I was young. I was academically ungifted. My climb up the corporate ladder didn't start until well into my thirties. The majority of my success was being in the right place at the right time and having mentors who took a chance on me. As a result, I have had a variety of roles that have given me exposure to broad aspects of the business world—technology, investing, marketing, sales, merchandising, product management, philanthropy, and managing continuous change. Paralleling my business career, I also found my two avocations: golf and writing. It still surprises me that I was able to become a senior corporate executive and play the top one-hundred ranked golf courses in the world. Imposter syndrome, I believe it's called.

It wasn't until I was forced to stop working because of some debilitating health problems that I had the chance to allow that seed planted all those years ago to grow into something bigger. It was time to better understand what was behind my attraction.

Most of us don't give much thought to what goes into making the Masters special. We find it compelling, but the afterglow wears off in a few days, and we go back to our lives. After attending the Masters numerous times, playing the course with two green jacket winners, and touring the clubhouse, I have given a lot of thought to not only what makes it special, but why.

There have been dozens of books written about the Masters. Most are from the perspective of the golf played during the tournament, or are about the course, or the history of the club and its founders. None have been written about what goes on behind the scenes to make it unique. What Augusta National has achieved shouldn't be surprising. For almost a hundred years, the membership has been comprised of three hundred of the smartest and most successful people from around the world, bound together by a common affinity for golf. And with a singular aim of producing the best sporting event in the world.

I had no access to Augusta National leadership, employees, or members as I wrote this book. Their invaluable brain trust operates behind closed doors, as is their right as a private club. As a result, I set out to reverse engineer their operating philosophies.

After closely looking at the history of the Masters and Augusta National, I identified ten principles that make it the special place it is. The ten principles are:

Principle #1     Exercise Restraint
Principle #2     Focus on the Details
Principle #3     Don't Be Overly Commercial
Principle #4     Use Technology Wisely
Principle #5     Adopt a Mindset of Continuous Improvement
Principle #6     Treat People with Respect
Principle #7     Cultivate Civility
Principle #8     Be Generous
Principle #9     Respect Tradition and Honor the Past
Principle #10    Use Scarcity to Create Value

As I was identifying the ten principles, the best way for me to understand why they resonated was to contrast them against the practices of other businesses and organizations, and of societal behavior in general. As I did, it became clear that their principles are largely the antithesis of how our world operates today. It is often stunning to see how badly degraded the norms we accept are, until we step back and compare them to the gold standard the Masters has created.

The beauty of the principles is that they have broad applicability. They can be applied to any business across any industry—be it a manufacturer, a retailer, or a services company. Likewise, regardless of personality type, the principles can also be used by individuals. The book was written to answer the question that has lingered since my first visit to Augusta National: *why can't the world be more like the Masters?*

# CHAPTER ONE

# Visionary Founders Establish the Culture

Tiger Woods is one of the most celebrated athletes of the last thirty years, ranking among the greatest golfers of all time. His impact ripples far beyond golf.

Before there was Tiger…there was another golfer who also transcended the game and changed it forever.

Given a blank sheet of paper and asked to conjure up a golf legend, it would be hard to imagine an individual as revered, smart, talented, and honorable as Bobby Jones. Among Jones's gifts was an underappreciated intellect. He graduated from high school at sixteen, earned a degree in mechanical engineering at Georgia Tech at twenty, a degree in English literature from Harvard two years later, then attended Emory School of Law for only three semesters, learning enough to master the law and pass the bar. Yet, when *Time* called him Atlanta's Boy Wonder, they were referring not to his brainpower, but to his ability to play golf.

He could play the game like few before or after. In the seven-year span between 1923 and 1929, he won the U.S. Open three times, the U.S. Amateur four times, and the

British Open twice. If we were to evaluate his career through the end of 1929, he would rank as one of the greatest of all time. And yet, his best year was still ahead. Jones won the "impregnable quadrilateral" in 1930, something that has only been accomplished once in the history of the sport, capturing all the big tournaments an amateur was eligible to play at the age of twenty-eight. Jones retired from competitive golf after 1930 because championship golf took a toll on him.

In the official ranking of golfers who have won the most major championships, Jones ranks seventh, although this understates his achievements. Because he remained an amateur his entire competitive career, he never competed in the PGA Championship, a self-imposed stricture limiting his ability to win more major championships. When making comparisons, it is important to remember that Jones was a part-time golfer. For many of the years he competed, he had to come out of "retirement" to play. Jones never played a full tournament schedule, spending most of his time on his schooling, his law practice, and his family.

In the last twelve Opens (the U.S. and the British) he entered, he won seven of them. Over the thirteen years he took part in major championships, he was a student for nine of them—it's no wonder he was lionized in the press from coast to coast from an early age. Over those same thirteen years, he took part in fifty-two tournaments, winning twenty-three, an unparalleled winning percentage of 44 percent. A member of the World Golf Hall of Fame, Jones was the second American awarded the Freedom of the City and Royal Burgh of St. Andrews, Scotland. Benjamin Franklin was the first.

His tournament record only tells part of the story. A man of honor, Jones called two penalties on himself in U.S.

Opens after his ball moved even though no one else could see the rules infraction. One was in 1925 and the other in 1926. The 1925 U.S. Open ended in a tie, and if Jones hadn't called the penalty on himself, he would have won. When congratulated about the incident and his honesty, Jones said, "There is only one way to play the game. You might as well praise a man for not robbing a bank."

The dean of sports writers, Herbert Warren Wind, who coined the term "Amen Corner," had a knack for assessing golfers—and for nailing their essence. He said about Jones, "Of all the people I have met in sports—or out—Jones came the closest to being what we call a great man. Like Winston Churchill, he had the quality of being at the same time much larger than life and exceedingly human."

Despite his stardom, Jones put golf in its proper perspective throughout his life. In one of the last interviews he gave, he said, "My wife and my children came first, then my profession. Finally, and never in a life by itself, came golf."

His legacy as a co-founder of Augusta National, and the Masters, is one of imparting civility, honesty, and respect into the tournament.

While Jones is a near-mythic figure, his Augusta National co-founder was a more complex and contradictory man. Called variously cantankerous, a dictator, stubborn, all-controlling, and a bastard, Clifford Roberts was a Wall Street man. Roberts was born in Iowa to parents who struggled with money, health issues, and emotional problems. Roberts and his brother worked at a variety of jobs—raising animals, milking cows, and caddying—to pay for their clothing and schoolbooks. While Jones graduated from high school at sixteen, Roberts dropped out at the same age. He enlisted in the Army Medical Corps during the First World War, and his training was fortuitously at Camp Hancock in Augusta. After the war, he eventually moved to New York. His fortunes waxed and waned through the years, particularly during the Stock Market Crash of 1929 and the Great Depression. It took two decades for him to become a one-sixth partner at Reynolds & Co. (which in future years would merge with Dean Witter and is today part of Morgan Stanley). Jones and Roberts met in New York in the mid-1920s and became friends.

Roberts never went to college and had a prickly temperament, particularly when contrasted to that of gentleman Jones. Despite his lack of polish and a compulsive personality, he had several strong suits, among them his focus, organizational skills, and attention to detail.

The Augusta National story begins with a nursery and an antebellum mansion. In 1857, Louis Mathieu Edouard Berckmans purchased four hundred acres in Augusta on the site of a failed indigo plantation. The plantation included a manor house, which is the current Augusta National clubhouse. Louis formed a nursery with his son, Prosper Jules Alphonse (P.J.A.), calling it Fruitlands—the largest in the South. They imported hundreds of varieties of trees and plants from around the world—popularizing azaleas in this country—and they planted a row of magnolia seeds along both sides of the driveway leading up to the manor house, which grew into what we now call Magnolia Lane.

Augusta National Golf Club was formed in 1931 and originally had a goal of recruiting eighteen hundred members. Jones and Roberts both spent considerable time and energy attempting to recruit members, but because they were doing so during the Great Depression, they were minimally successful. After sending out thousands of invitations soliciting memberships across the country, their recruitment efforts fell far, far, short of their goals. The most exclusive club operating today opened with a fizzle, rather than a bang. They had fewer than one hundred members. The course's official opening was in 1933.

Serendipity often plays a role in bringing people together, putting them in the right place at the right time. Roberts's training for the Army just happened to be in Augusta, a spot Jones had visited to play golf during the winter months, establishing a connection they would build on after they met. Jones and Roberts somehow perfectly complemented each other, providing just the right elements to make the Masters the perfection that it is. "Bobby Jones had a way of looking at the world from high above, like an eagle, viewing life in a grand manner," wrote Charles Price, author of a biography about Jones titled, *A Golf Story*. Price came to know Jones well, and his analysis is clear and perceptive: "Nobody but Jones could have brought off such an enterprise—the trinity of club, course, and tournament." He continued, "Cliff Roberts, on the other hand, reveled in ground-level details, at which he was a master, often implementing Jones's ambitious ideas to tiny degrees Jones had not the patience for." The long-time producer of the Masters television broadcast on CBS echoed the sentiment. "Jones was the soul of the Masters and Roberts was the body. Bob didn't have much to do with the nuts and bolts of the operation; he was a spiritual leader."

Bobby Jones was an impeccable dresser who retained his boyish good looks throughout his life; he was an eloquent speaker who studied Shakespeare. Cliff Roberts wore large glasses and his ears stuck out; he was gravel-throated, and his speaking style was choppy. Augusta National's co-founders were an odd couple that turned out to be the perfect combination, a duo that nurtured the Masters into the best sporting event in the world.

Curt Sampson, the author of *The Masters: Golf, Money and Power in Augusta, Georgia*, sums up Cliff Roberts's management style in three crisp sentences: "At the club's first meeting, it was decided that there would be no more meetings. Augusta National would be an autocracy. He wielded power like the Old Testament God, with lots of rules—and no mercy." Roberts's co-founder was more hands-off, and his impact on the Masters was subtler, but equally important. "The aura for the tournament belonged solely to Bobby Jones," winner of the 1935 Masters, Gene Sarazen, said, "He was the reason we all came to play."

The underlying principles that make the Masters the special event it is aren't written down like the Ten Commandments. However, the Gospel According to Cliff and Bob is simple and easy to understand. Their governing philosophies have become enshrined in the club because the leadership has treated them as core principles, staying true to the ideas and actions of the founders. It's one of the intangibles that great organizations share—a strong, self-reinforcing, self-perpetuating culture.

Looking beneath Roberts's gruff exterior, there was a striking vision of what the Masters should be. He writes at the end of his book, *The Story of Augusta National*, that the Masters was established with a singularity of purpose, which was to benefit the game of golf: "I would like in conclusion to make the observation that those with talent who give unselfishly of themselves just because they love golf are entitled to one uncomplicated place where they can feel completely at ease."

# CHAPTER TWO

# A Master Class in Branding

The best investments can come from the unlikeliest places. An astute millennial in suburban Georgia followed the most basic of investment axioms: buy low, sell high. He was rewarded with a return on his investment that made even the smartest hedge fund managers look like amateurs.

In the spring of '24, a green garden gnome was put up for auction with little fanfare. Bidding began calmly enough. Drawn in by the perfect packaging and a pristine condition, an influx of buyers rushed in. The auction finished in a flourish, with fifty bids placed. When the hammer fell, the mythical creature sold for a whopping $8,900. The seller paid only $39.50 for the little man eight years before. He gained 22,431 percent on his investment.

The gnome was so sought after because he was adorned with a Masters logo on his sweater and his cap. It transformed his value and offers a lesson in the value of branding. The classic role of a gnome is to guard gold and treasures, yet that little logo elevated him into a treasure. The Masters had unwittingly created one of the greatest investment vehicles of our time. The Masters logo—a yellow and green outline of the continental United States with a red golf flag sticking out of a cup at the course location—is simple yet elegant. Like the Nike Swoosh and the Olympic rings, it is iconic and recognized by people from Kokomo to Korea. It is the mark of a respected brand.

How did we get to the point where a one-foot-high statue, patterned after a fairy-tale dwarfish figure, and designed to sit among petunias, became worth so much? Granted, the chubby little bloke is cute. His face is aglow with rosy cheeks, an endearing smile, a fancy mustache, a well-trimmed beard, and bushy white eyebrows. The tournament's Instagram account announced his maiden arrival on April 6, 2016: "There is a new visitor to #themasters this year," with a crisp image of the newly minted curio. The diminutive fellow that achieved the record price is something collectors of every ilk seek out: a first edition in mint condition.

I will leave it to the reader to determine whether the buyer has more money than brains, or whether this was a brilliant purchase akin to buying an early Warhol. The small-town Georgia seller wasn't the only one making a small fortune. Three other 2016 gnomes sold for $7,000 each on eBay a week earlier.

The craze for Masters items is not limited to gnomes, although they are the most noteworthy. People around the world wear Masters shirts, hats, and other gear with pride. There is a certain amount of boasting that goes along with wearing Masters-logoed items, but also satisfaction in being affiliated with an organization that has high standards and an increasingly rare quality—class. The Masters merchandise operation is one viewed with envy by retailers, selling an estimated $69 million in branded goods in one week. Patrons behave like it's Black Friday every day at Augusta National. Every hour the gates are open, the tournament sells roughly $1 million in logoed goods. The brand is so powerful they put the logo on hundreds of items, including women's scarfs and pullovers, pajamas, clocks, footballs, tote bags, T-shirts, watches, beer koozies, coffee mugs, belts, backpacks, dog collars, piggy banks, posters, teddy bears, and onesies for newborns.

Not to imply they are haphazard about their product selections—quite to the contrary, and consistent with their brand, whatever they put a Masters logo on is tastefully done.

How and why the gnome became such a sought-after item is a mystery unto itself. Understanding the vagaries of the consumer and what they will buy is an art form few can predict in advance. Whether through luck or skill, or a combination of the two, the gnomes are now a phenomenon. They are a microcosm of the Masters in a neat package— desirable, tastefully done, produced in exquisite detail, marketed in a technologically savvy way, and without a hint of crassness. They have an aura about them and are emblematic of the power of the Masters and their brand.

Anyone lucky enough to have attended the Masters inevitably comments on several things:

1. How everything is perfect; every inch of the property is meticulous, manicured, and beautiful.
2. How inexpensive the food and drinks are; and how it feels good not to get gouged.

3. How jaw-dropping the golf shop operation is to see firsthand.

4. How well-mannered everyone is—both the folks that work there and the patrons. Even the attendants in the restrooms!

Those who have only watched on television are typically impressed with:

1. How rejuvenating it is to see the flawless green grass and colorful azaleas as we are coming out of winter.

2. How refreshing it is to watch a sports program without the broadcasters babbling continually.

3. How nice it is not to be bombarded with commercials.

4. How comforting and soothing the timeless Masters theme song is—the Masters is a reawakening of the senses and an anticipated ritual to mark the beginning of spring, and if a season can have a theme song, this is it.

The mystique of the Masters didn't happen by accident. It is a carefully cultivated and highly orchestrated event. The aura took decades to perfect and is part of an ecosystem guided by Augusta National that has a strict set of rules and guardrails to ensure that everything is done in a first-class manner. It takes immense skill and a singular focus to achieve perfection, and few do; but to do it in such a way that the reasons behind it aren't entirely obvious is especially difficult. Michelangelo worked on David for more than three years. The skill and effort required to sculpt a big block of stone into the perfection that he did is hard to fully comprehend. What makes it engrossing? Is it the massive size? Or the detailing, like the pulsing veins on the back of the hands? The smoothness of the Carrara marble, or something else that is difficult to nail down? It is a complex answer.

The same is true of the Masters.

The members of Augusta National will tell us they have achieved nowhere near the level of perfection they desire, and as we will see, that is one of the intangibles that makes the Masters alluring.

Although the Masters represents something special, I believe Augusta National's principles can be replicated. By distilling down the essence of how the club has cultivated and molded the Masters into the exalted brand it has become, the lessons become clear. Once understood, it also becomes clear how other businesses can shape and improve their brands in a similar fashion. And, how individuals can also adopt some of their clever approaches to enhance their personal brands.

The elephant in the room when discussing the Masters and Augusta National is money. They have boatloads of it. Undoubtedly, it would be easy to replicate some of their formula with unlimited funds. Yet, as the reader will discover, money isn't always necessary to emulate their wizardry. Paradoxically, downplaying money has increased the value of their brand. Kyle Porter, formerly of CBS Sports, who writes the *Normal Sport* newsletter, has studied the Masters for years. He notes that they leave a substantial amount of money on the table by keeping ticket and food prices low, and how this helps them control their brand: "Because to the Masters, nothing — not money in the short or long term — is as important as its brand. This is not the choice every business makes because it takes tremendous discipline."

I found several surprises as I performed a deep dive of the Masters. A witty and entertaining TikTok slideshow the club posted during the 2024 Masters is titled, "A day like gnome other." It contains twenty images of the 2024 version of the gnome strung together, mimicking a patron's experience attending the tournament and moving around the course. One image shows him standing in a concession area in front of a rack stuffed with bags of Masters-logoed potato chips, captioned, "Snacks!!!!" It's probably safe to assume that the serious and accomplished members of Augusta National have never used four exclamation points to emphasize something. It's only a thing for members of certain generations who grew up in an emotive technology world.

Embracing TikTok and issuing a new limited-edition gnome each year. What's going on here? I highlight it because it demonstrates how a bunch of rich members, perceived as stodgy, are also adaptive and innovative, quietly using technology in sophisticated and surprising ways. The tournament is rooted in tradition, but as we will explore, another part of their ethos is to constantly innovate.

Before looking at the principles in detail, let's briefly explore what it's like to attend the Masters.

# CHAPTER THREE

# The Masters Experience

Some people can remember elaborate details about their childhood and tell colorful stories.

I don't remember much about mine.

My father was a civil servant his whole life and trying to raise six boys on his meager income meant we didn't take vacations. The first time I experienced Disney World was when I took my kids. One of the few recollections I have of my early years was going on field trips in grade school. Living in North Jersey, fifteen miles from Times Square, meant our field trips were often to New York City. I especially remember when our class visited the Bronx Zoo.

I have such good memories of field trips because there was a sense of adventure and possibility while on them—they were a time of delight. It was a chance to get out of my myopic middle-class cocoon and experience the world.

The zoo is a sprawling land of exploration, 265 acres accessed via an ornate set of bronze Art Deco gates. The environment includes grandly designed Beaux-Arts buildings, a historic Italian Fountain, and river views. As a child, I knew little about architectural styles or animals that live in the African savanna. It was the way I *felt* that was memorable— the innate sense of wonder and joy that kids have.

One of the primary reasons the Masters resonates when you attend is because it is one of the few experiences that makes you feel that sense of fascination and happiness. Growing older opens its own possibilities and experiences, but the childhood sense of wonder is worn away—we find out that the Easter Bunny and the Tooth Fairy aren't real. And we learn that bad things happen: people die, hearts break from lost loves, red tape and politics make us jaded, we experience a boss who is an incompetent buffoon—leaving us with a sense of cynicism.

The Masters is a chance to return to what life was like before we learned about Murphy's law and the law of the jungle.

There is no substitute for going to the Masters in person. It is enlightening and should be a life goal for any fan of golf, regardless of how casual. This is easier said than done, and for most, experiencing it firsthand means winning a ticket in the annual Masters lottery.

"Welcome to the Masters." The pleasant greeting is first heard at the approach to the entry gates, and over and over again winding through the entry process—from the security guards, the greeters, and from members of Augusta National wearing their green jackets.

We've all seen Masters winners wearing their green jackets on television, in pictures posted online, and in magazines. When each year's tournament winner receives his green jacket, there are scores of members sitting in chairs behind the ceremony wearing their green jackets. En masse, they are intimidating and have the same look as the College of Cardinals sitting in the Sistine Chapel—the outfit accords a sense of formality and respect; a recognition that they have achieved something worth achieving. And a separation from the rest of us. The uniform is a signal to the world: *I am different.*

Being greeted by an Augusta National member in the flesh wearing their green jacket has an outsized impact. It is an indication that you have arrived at a special place.

In a day full of revelations, the security operation is one to marvel at. It is the anti-TSA. The security personnel aren't screaming, there are no passive-aggressive shows of power—they are high-spirited, and the lines move along at a rapid pace. I find myself returning to that nagging question: if the Masters can do this well, why can't others? As the day progresses, it won't be the last time the thought returns. While waiting to go through security, the perfection that personifies the Masters starts to unfold. It begins with the clusters of well-manicured flowers sitting atop mounds. There are little white cabins dotted around. Something about their proportions and how they fit into the landscape feels right.

Once through security, you are carried along by the crowd through winding paths and banks of flowers. The heart starts to race a little. Then, more hillsides filled with pink and white flowers in full bloom appear.

Walking another two or three hundred yards, the confines of the floral corridor opens to the expanse of the driving range. The murmur of superlatives patrons have been uttering since going through security now rises to a chorus: *Wow…No way…This is perfect…Oh my God…You've got to be kidding me.* Or veteran attendees can be overheard explaining the nuances to those who have made the pilgrimage for the first time: *Try to find a weed or a blade of grass out of place…I told you…You have to see it to believe it.* It's not just the average patron who has these reactions. While attending for the first time, Wayne Gretzky's reaction was, "Wow, died and gone to heaven." Former U.S. Open champion Geoff Ogilvy remarked it was "the prettiest place in the world." Arnold Palmer said on his first visit, "When I got here, I felt like I was walking on a cloud."

The Masters calls the walkway between the driving range and the first fairway the Patron Corridor, and it is one of the few places on the property where there are throngs of people. The Corridor is shaded, set under a canopy of tall trees. Exiting the tree cover and spilling back into the daylight provides a moment that sears into the memory. The expanse of the golf course is now in full view.

The first hole has a dramatic twenty-foot-deep ravine in the initial part of the fairway. The par-five second is a stunner, sweeping down into the valley floor. Walking down the second fairway is an education at Augusta National; it is littered with azaleas beneath the loblolly pines, and the contrast of their delicate pink flowers set below the towering trees is stunning. After an hour or two, it begins to sink in how nice everyone at the Masters is—there are nothing but smiles and well-mannered behaviors throughout the day. People understand what a privilege it is to be on property, and it shows. There is something Zen about the experience— politeness breeds politeness, and the contagion effect is real. The Japanese have an expression, "The nail that sticks up gets hammered down," which is a social metaphor for following the norms or being ostracized. Unobtrusive public behavior and conformity are self-reinforced at the Masters, and it is a rarity to find a boorish fan. Those who can't be happy and well-behaved in this environment have something wrong with them.

The grandstand above the eighth green is a good place to rest and a fine place to watch the creativity of short game shots. I was taught early on to avoid making eye contact while riding the subway in New York City. Keep to yourself, don't talk to anyone, avoid trouble—keep your body language closed, and your valuables hidden. The grandstands at the Masters are the antithesis of that. Everybody is convivial and natural conversations are struck up with great ease. It's sad that as we have become increasingly tribal and self-isolating, it's hard to see what we've lost. By asking us to put away our cell phones and abide by their long-standing traditions, the Masters allows us to interact with one another again and share a communal experience. No one seems to care if you are liberal or conservative, a surgeon or a mechanic. We are bound only by our love of the game and our respect for the tournament.

Amen Corner should be seen in succession to fully appreciate its drama. The exacting approach shot to the eleventh green, with the pond looming on the left, is where competitors start to pray to themselves. Walking down the eleventh fairway offers the first in-person glimpse of Rae's Creek and the Hogan and Nelson bridges, the spectacle of twelve, and the glorious panorama of the most famous three-hole stretch in golf. "There's no bigger thrill in golf than the walk from Augusta National's eleventh green to the twelfth tee," Fred Couples, the 1992 Masters champion, has said.

The Garden of Eden is now fully in view.

The thirteenth hole is the prettiest in the world. More than fifteen hundred azaleas help to create the picture-perfect backdrop, beginning with the azaleas tumbling down the hillside from the tee. The tilting fairway that falls into the rocky creek is lined with azaleas bursting in seasonal color, sitting under the canopies of the tall pines.

The grandstand adjacent to the fourteenth tee is the garden spot on the property, both physically and metaphorically. Besides providing a front row seat to watch balls sail into the air from the tee, the elevation allows the most mesmerizing view of the thirteenth. A sense of contentment is sure to wash over even the grouchiest among us, especially on a day when a warm sun washes over the grandstand. This spot, more than any other on the course, brings me back to my childhood, and that unadulterated joy of seeing the world through a kid's eyes again. Seeing it up close elicits an emotional response, and it begins to explain why a Masters ticket is such a coveted prize. It's the same reason it is satisfying to take kids to Disneyland—that elation. I fondly remember tearing up watching my daughter hugging Cinderella and being the happiest she has ever been.

I am fortunate to have traveled widely, and I've seen some of the prettiest places on the planet: Sydney Harbor, with its postcard views and crystal-clear water; Cape Town, South Africa, with Table Mountain towering above; the Vatican; the majestic Scottish Highlands; the awe-inspiring peaks on the South Island of New Zealand; Venice viewed from the Grand Canal; the manicured gardens of Kyoto, and the mysterious Mount Fuji; the Grand Canyon, and Big Sur. Beauty is in the eye of the beholder, but for me, being in this little corner of Georgia, soaking in the thirteenth hole on a seasonable day when a new season is in the air, beats them all.

The active crosswalk in the middle of the fifteenth fairway is typically abuzz with crisscrossing patrons visualizing golf shots out loud. Without the distractions of a cell phone, the mind is free to play imaginary shots all day, with patrons in the present. The lack of disturbances is one of the keys that make Augusta National the peaceful dreamworld it is.

The 365 acres of Augusta National are full of adults being the happiest they can be. That's the Masters experience.

The sixteenth grandstand is one of the prime places to take in all the tournament has to offer. The view of tee shots on sixteen is up close and personal, with a full view of the tee and the green. The grandstand is the ideal location to sit and watch the world go by, with a bonus—food and drinks are nearby. The food operation runs with the same efficiency as the rest of the Masters. And the workers serving the food and running the cash registers are chipper. Each and every one.

The sixteenth is one of the spots on the course that screams "spring!" Not only from the brilliance of the floral display, but also from the splash of colors created by patrons encircling the pond. The soft yellows, lime greens, pinks, fuchsias, baby blues, turquoises, and whites—seen under a deep blue sky, in the natural amphitheater wrapping around the pond—is as good a picture of springtime as exists. On a day when the crowds are thick, it is acre after acre of soothing colors offset by the vivid green grass circling the water. The picture is intensified because the colors reflect off the dark pond, doubling the impact.

Although some badge holders at the Masters are granted access to the clubhouse or the corporate hospitality pavilion known as Berckmans Place, everyone feels privileged to be on the property. The environment is egalitarian because all patrons have access to the entire course, and the behavioral norms apply to everyone. "There are rules designed to create the best tournament experience in the world," Brendan Porath writes in *The Fried Egg*. He continues, "And this is the one place almost everyone follows them, regardless of their Instagram follower count or title or tax bracket."

Returning year after year, the Masters never loses its luster; in fact, because of the governing philosophy of how it is operated, it gets better each time. In a world full of travel disappointments and experiences that let us down because they are overhyped and overrated, the Masters is bigger and better than imagined. Attending the Masters is captivating because it is a rare opportunity to experience life in a bubble, with the worries, stresses, and inconveniences of life in the background. Even though it is ephemeral, one of the reasons it is such a sought-after experience is because capturing that feeling, if only just for a day or a week, is so difficult to do.

The wealthy have the privilege of creating their own bubbles, living in cloistered enclaves: Bel-Air, Boulder, and Beverly Hills; Aspen and Atherton; Park City and Palm Beach; Sausalito and Santa Barbara; Rancho Santa Fe and Rye; the Hamptons. College campuses allow young adults to experience bubbles in all their glory. Private prep schools are the very definition of a bubble.

As with many things, the Brits do it better than us, and their academic bubbles at Eton, Harrow, Oxford, and Cambridge are best-in-breed. A good rule of thumb is that if you're somewhere with a quadrangle, you're in a bubble (interestingly, Augusta National refers to its property as a campus). As far as experiential bubbles, Las Vegas qualifies, although with a focus on debauchery. Any of the Disney theme parks are bubbles.

Aspiring to be inside a bubble is undoubtedly a First World objective. And since it is unlikely most of us will return to college, or have the money to live like the top one percent, the Masters is a golden place to experience it. The sense of camaraderie among those lucky enough to attend is real, and leaving the elegant bubble is always painful.

# CHAPTER FOUR

# The Ten Principles that Create the Magic

It was a startup that made Listerine commercials and worked on medical imagery. Their rented office space near Oakland was "in the shadow of a refinery." Burlington Northern freight trains would thunder by so close that those working there could almost reach out and touch them. Dogs roamed the halls.

From these humble beginnings, Pixar changed the rules of the game. *Toy Story* was their first feature film, produced with a budget of $30 million. Their unlikely formula for success: throw together a jumble of computer scientists, artists, filmmakers, and screenwriters. Add in movie star voiceovers. And . . .

A new genre was born—the computer-animated feature film.

Their combination of ingredients was magic. The whole was clearly greater than the sum of its parts, with the *Toy Story* franchise grossing over $4 billion and still going strong.

Likewise, Augusta National has its own magic formula, where the whole is also greater than the sum of its parts. Not Hollywood-style magic, but a unique and well-honed form of Southern magic. While each of the ten principles Augusta National uses is important, and each presents a stand-alone learning opportunity, it is the combination of them working together that makes the Masters the Masters.

It is their secret sauce.

**Contrasting the Masters with Other Organizations**

Over the coming chapters, we will look in detail at each of the principles, and after each principle, I dedicate a chapter to businesses that also use some of the principles. I find it is a helpful method to highlight what can be learned from Augusta National. It helps to crystallize best practices. It also helps to explain why those organizations highlighted have achieved greater levels of success or admiration than others. Some appear to be unlikely comparisons at first, but when looked at beneath the surface, the similarities reveal themselves. While each of the chosen organizations is aligned with only one principle, many were chosen because they also embody other principles in the way they operate.

As I looked at organizations that also excelled by using some of the principles the Masters uses, I found common elements among them. There is a big divide between how we are treated by large companies (generally poorly) and how we are treated by small businesses (generally well). Except for the military, it is widely acknowledged that government entities aren't well run and treat us poorly. No one looks to the IRS, TSA, or the post office and tries to model their business practices after them, but that is precisely what many big businesses have done.

Although my sample size is small, I also found that ownership structure matters in how customers are regarded, with a noticeable difference between publicly traded companies and those owned by private equity (generally bad), and those that are private companies or employee-owned (generally good).

Sometimes my analysis of the current environment—and companies—is highly critical. This is because I believe we learn just as much by looking at what's wrong as what's right. The contrasts are sharper than only praising what works.

## The Masters Transcends Golf

The Masters television broadcast reaches from Andorra to Zanzibar—190 countries in total. Even the 11,151 souls on Wallis, a remote atoll in the middle of the Pacific, can watch the Masters. Tiger Woods aptly notes, "Everyone knows what the Masters is, even if you're a non-golfer. People know what Wimbledon is. They know what the Super Bowl is. There are certain events that people just know about." It transcends golf because of the way they gracefully weave together their ten magical principles into an event that is known and admired the world over.

## Why?

One of the fascinating things about kids is their inquisitiveness. Their curiosity is as endless as their question asking. Without any awareness, they repeatedly ask "why?"

As we mature, our egos get in the way, and we stop asking an endless series of questions because it might make us look daft. I have approached the book through the eyes of a kid and their curiosity, asking an endless set of questions. Why isn't the world more like the Masters? Why can't we learn to do things the way they do? Why is it that the Masters transcends golf?

Let's explore the principles and understand why they strike such a chord.

# CHAPTER FIVE

# Principle #1

# Exercise Restraint

The Masters television broadcast has been shaped by the hand of two autocratic leaders. And by the many rules dictated by Augusta National. While current leadership is gentler stylistically, they remain strict about their rules. The history of the broadcast is a lesson in both the value of following rules and exercising restraint.

It is unpopular today to praise autocratic leadership styles. Feel-good management is in the vanguard. Only a masochist wants to work with a boss who is domineering and doesn't take input from others. Gaining a consensus and getting the viewpoint of as many constituents as possible leads to better decisions—the wisdom of the crowd.

Or, the dreaded management by committee, depending upon your perspective.

While reading this chapter, I would ask the reader to suspend any preconceived notions about autocratic vs.

inclusive management styles. Occasionally, having a driven, visionary leader who is difficult to deal with can lead to greatness. Steve Jobs is the classic example. Charles Price felt the same was true of Augusta National's co-founder: "Cliff Roberts was, in the last analysis, an autocrat in the absolute, and that is what all golf clubs and all golf tournaments need above anything else if they are going to venture into the extraordinary."

The Masters television broadcast began to differentiate itself when a colorful character entered the scene. The Augusta National co-founders were joined in their pursuit of excellence by a foul-mouthed, chain-smoking, impatient Armenian-American named Frank Chirkinian. Chirkinian got his big break in 1959 when he was asked to produce the nascent Masters broadcast for CBS at age thirty-three. It was a job he would hold for thirty-eight years. Chirkinian turned out to be a fortuitous choice because he shared two key traits with Cliff Roberts—he was an innovator and a dictator. He had strong ideas about what would make televised golf compelling, and he expressed those ideas in a candid and direct fashion.

Jones also gave him sage advice, "Frank, the more golf you show, the better your product is." It was a philosophy he would use his entire career, taking it to an extreme for the benefit of fans: "When I die, I want my epitaph to read, 'He stayed out of the way.'" Chirkinian told *Sports Illustrated* that Jones gave him another mandate: "He said, never mention money during a Masters telecast. Money is not the point of golf. Please don't talk about it."

Roberts and Chirkinian jousted about the broadcasts often, with Roberts sending a meticulously detailed letter to

CBS every year, critiquing their work. Like many of his relationships, Roberts's relationship with the network was complicated. He referred to the media as "our news fraternity friends," yet he wanted to control every aspect of the television production. *Sports Illustrated* noted that he "used more muscle and less finesse, often resorting to finger-jabbing the chests of CBS Sports executives as he laid down the law." He wanted very limited advertising and insisted there be no breaks for local stations. It was a relationship that worked perfectly for Chirkinian, who confessed, "Cliff Roberts taught me everything I know about being an autocrat."

Viewers of the Masters relish in the sense of calm the broadcast has, a key way it sets itself apart from other broadcasts—not only in golf, but throughout sports. Watching the Masters is a de-stressing activity of the highest order—the sporting equivalent of watching Bob Ross paint. In one of his annual letters to CBS, Roberts wrote, "I think too much chatty conversation by a commentator as a part of a golf tournament show is the worst thing of all. The main thing the golfing fan wants is understandable and accurate information."

Vin Scully served as the anchor of the broadcast from 1975 through 1982, and he was a good choice. Scully's lyrical style was ideal for the sport. Arguably the greatest sports announcer of all time, Scully broadcast Dodger games for sixty-seven years. He knew when to speak, and when not to, "Day to day, week in, week out. If something happens and the crowd roars, I shut up," Scully famously said.

It is the same philosophy still followed by the Masters broadcast. His soothing, even demeanor, punctuated by pauses, allowed viewers to watch the action unfold on screen in an unhurried fashion. Contrary to the current standard of sports broadcasting, the world doesn't stop spinning if there are a few seconds, or longer, of silence, and it is part of what makes it so pleasant to watch. When *GOLF* magazine surveyed its readers, asking what their favorite tournament to watch was, 86 percent said it was the Masters.

The English golf journalist and broadcaster Henry Longhurst called the action from the sixteenth hole for many years. Longhurst's voice was soft, speaking barely above a whisper. A one-time member of the British Parliament, he wrote extensively about the game, bringing historical context to his commentary. He said what made the broadcast so good were the "brilliant flashes of silence." Ben Wright, who commentated on the fifteenth hole for many years, said that Chirkinian told him, "I've got a piece of advice for you that you'd be well advised to take to heart. We're nothing but caption writers in the picture business. And if you can't improve the pictures with your best-chosen words, keep your mouth shut." Longhurst and Wright were excellent choices, knowledgeable and succinct, their English accents adding a touch of class that Americans love.

"De-emphasize the players' antics"—one of thirty-three rules that govern the CBS broadcast of the Masters. Not following the rules of the broadcast has severe repercussions, even for commentators whose overall shtick was humor. "I don't think they mow these greens," Gary McCord said during the 1994 broadcast, "I think they bikini wax them." CBS kicked McCord off future broadcasts. Precision of language is also important, and words to use are prescribed in detail to the broadcasters—patrons, not fans; first nine and second nine, instead of front nine and back nine; bunkers, not sand traps;

and the water in front of the thirteenth green is not called Rae's Creek, but a tributary of Rae's Creek.

The Masters has only four television sponsors in the U.S., who air limited commercials to offset production costs. CBS and ESPN (which airs the tournament on Thursday and Friday) pay nothing to broadcast the golf. The agreement between the club and the broadcasters is a "year-to-year handshake agreement," giving Augusta National the leverage it desires. The limited commercial interruptions are without a doubt one of the elements that gives the Masters that X-factor.

Since the broadcast has so few commercial interruptions, picking best-in-breed broadcasters is of paramount importance to CBS. The executives running the broadcast should be praised for the adroitness of their picks. Some of fans' fondest memories of the Masters are the iconic calls made by the first-class CBS broadcast team. The genial Verne Lundquist is the perfect example.

As Jack Nicklaus was surging for an unlikely and unprecedented sixth green jacket at the age of forty-six, he made an eagle on the fifteenth hole. Jim Nantz, the current host of the program, made one of his best calls ever on the sixteenth. As Nicklaus lined up his putt for birdie and the ball rolled in, there was a pause for a full eight seconds. It was classic CBS Masters. And then the setup line, "And there's no doubt about it." Followed by another trademark Nantz pause, before uttering, "The Bear has come out of hibernation." On the next hole, Nicklaus took a long time to line up his eighteen-foot putt to gain sole possession of the lead. As the ball approached the hole, Lundquist uttered in a low voice, "Maybe." And then after a second of silence, as the ball trickled into the front of the cup, a simple line that is forever etched into our memories, "Yes sir!"

The most famous Masters call of all time was on the sixteenth hole, as Tiger was en route to his fourth green jacket. Tiger had missed the green and lined up to intentionally play a wedge shot twenty-five feet away from the pin. He did what every golfer at every level dreams of doing. He hit the perfect shot. As the ball rolled toward the pin and looked like it was tracking to go in, Lundquist said, in his usual unpretentious style, "Oh my goodness!" And then, as the ball hung on the lip, unsure whether it was going to fall, Lundquist had the presence of mind to say nothing. After the ball rolled in, he went completely out of character and screamed at the top of his lungs, "OH WOW!" He then waited another six seconds before saying the defining words of his long and distinguished career, "In your life have you seen anything like that!" An underappreciated part of the call was that neither Lundquist nor anyone else on the broadcast team spoke for twenty-five seconds after the "in your life" call, punctuating it to perfection.

It was one of the greatest shots ever hit in golf with commentary to match.

Broadcasting sports at the highest level is an acquired skill, especially knowing when to be quiet. What elevates all three of these calls are not only the well-chosen words, but the fact that they were punctuated with silence before and after. It's a part of the Masters magic.

Although Chirkinian retired in 1996 and wasn't producing the program at the time of Tiger's shot, his successor, Lance Barrow, followed the same "stay out of the way" philosophy, as does the current producer, Sellers Shy. Their winning streak, picking the best talent, has continued, with knowledgeable, but not overbearing, commentators achieving just the right balance. Their penchant for former professionals with foreign accents has continued over the decades, with the exotic voices giving just the right flair. Having a green jacket winner as the lead analyst alongside Nantz is smart and adds immeasurably to the broadcast.

Aside from the minimalist approach to commercials and the understated manner of the broadcasters, two other elements make the Masters broadcast so devastatingly good. One is how they show off the splendor of the course periodically, using drones to take pictures from above, zooming in on flowers and shrubs bursting with color, or showing the majesty of Amen Corner. While there are lulls in the action, rather than cluttering up the broadcast with fluff or statistics, they choose to soothe instead, showing off their unfair advantage relative to other golf broadcasts: their unmatched beauty (although CBS's broadcasts from Pebble Beach get an honorable mention).

The final element is their music. Even casual fans, who don't know the difference between a smothered shot and a shank, perk up when they hear the Masters theme song.

The golden thread underlying the broadcast is simple—less is more. What isn't seen and heard is as important as what is. Less talking and fewer commercials. No bombast and no irreverence. What's difficult to understand is why more broadcasts don't emulate the approach. Golf suffers from the same affliction that many sports broadcasts do—too many statistics—a pitcher's spin rate, a homer's exit velocity, clubhead speed, launch angle. Understanding what sets a broadcast apart to a degree few ever have, Vin Scully wisely said, "Statistics are used much like a drunk uses a lamppost: for support, not illumination," precisely describing our frustration with the low quality of broadcasting today.

The Masters is thankfully the sane exception to the drought of excellent sports broadcasts. Some would call it old school, some would call it boring, but I think it resonates. After all, watching sports is a respite from the troubles and stresses of our lives. The endless pursuit of younger viewers who want action-packed golf broadcasts has had the opposite effect, turning off more viewers than it attracts.

How do we square the contradiction about an autocratic leadership style being a good way to achieve greatness? By choosing the best parts while discarding the toxic ones. Having a boss who launches a tirade of profanities at you or publicly embarrasses you is a thing of the past. Roberts and Chirkinian got away with it because they were of a different generation. Current and recent leadership of Augusta National still insist on having lots of rules, and they are strict about enforcing them. But they do it in a way that is respectful. The producers of the CBS broadcast who succeeded Chirkinian are still able to instill restraint into the broadcast, without resorting to a string of F-bombs directed at everyone in the booth.

In Frank Chirkinian's obituary in the *New York Times,* the headline was, "the father of televised golf," an apt moniker. Over his distinguished career, he earned four Emmys and two Peabody awards for his excellence in broadcasting. Chirkinian called Augusta National "the greatest theater in sports." It is a theater he helped to mythify by instilling a sense of restraint into his work.

As we look at each principle, I have included insights from members of Augusta National past and present to reinforce the principles and show the collective brainpower that the club has at its disposal.

| Lessons from Augusta National Members |
| --- |
| "We will continue to follow a policy of thoughtful restraint." – George Schultz, former U.S. Secretary of State and former Secretary of the Treasury |

# CHAPTER SIX

# How to Exercise Restraint

The Masters broadcast demonstrates how using restraint can lead to excellence. What about applying the idea more broadly? The California-based In-N-Out Burger is an excellent example that demonstrates how using restraint can lead to outsized success.

## In-N-Out Burger

The revered In-N-Out Burger: cheeseburger, hamburger, french fries, a Double-Double, shakes, and beverages. Those are the only menu choices (well, except the secret menu). In-N-Out is a shining example of a brand that takes a minimalist approach to all aspects of their business, and they have through-the-roof brand loyalty. Based on net promoter scores, In-N-Out ranks among the top fifteen brands in the world, with an 88 percent customer loyalty rating, higher than Ritz-Carlton or Tiffany and Co.

The company has always been restrained in its approach to growth. It will only open new locations when it has sufficiently trained managers to operate them within the company's exacting standards. In-N-Out and McDonald's started at roughly the same time, but because In-N-Out has intentionally restrained its growth to focus on quality, it has only one-tenth the number of stores as McDonald's. Some will look at that statistic and think, *I'd rather be McDonald's,* because they're bigger and make more money. It comes down to a philosophical question: focus on size and growth or focus on quality. McDonald's has made a nice return for its investors, but I'd rather eat at In-N-Out.

In-N-Out is also restrained in its use of technology. They play on a nostalgia theme and the California lifestyle on social media. Going against the norm, the company does not have an app that allows customers to order on their phones. They do this because they only want to serve the freshest possible food and feel the best way to achieve that is to have customers order at the drive-through or enter the store. No doubt they lose some sales by doing so, but counterintuitively, that restraint helps to reinforce a core part of their brand.

Their business has other similarities to how the Masters operates. They use a distinct language: animal style, the home run, the Flying Dutchman, four by four, and snowed. And like the Masters, their merchandise is worn as a show of pride. In-N-Out also lives by the sixth principle, respecting their associates by paying them above industry norms. A store manager makes more than $180,000 on average, including sharing in their store's profits.

Lynsi Snyder, the president of In-N-Out and the founder's granddaughter, talks proudly about how the company does no franchising and has no outside investors, saying, "Some things in life and business are more important than lining our pockets. Our loftiest goal is to consistently offer you the best."

In the same way that staying silent during a broadcast can create outsized value, the same is true when it is applied to our personal lives. It is a truism laid down by the Greek philosopher Epictetus thousands of years ago, and it represents a lost art: "We have two ears and one mouth so that we can listen twice as much as we speak."

Many leaders, particularly those who are Type-A, like to show how smart they are. They talk too much and need to have the last word. Restraint is often a better technique and suggests a sense of gravitas. It also demonstrates discipline. Those with more discipline generally make better leaders. It is a good example of how less is often more.

The same approach applies not only to the spoken word, but to our actions. It's sometimes more important what we don't do than what we do. Jim Collins, author of the bestselling book *Good to Great*, is a proponent of making "stop-doing" lists in addition to to-do lists. His idea is that if we stop doing things that won't have a meaningful impact, it creates more time to focus on things that do.

### Lessons from Augusta National Members

"The difference between successful people and really successful people is that really successful people say no to almost everything." – Warren Buffett

# CHAPTER SEVEN

# Principle #2

# Focus on the Details

Herbert Warren Wind wrote that Cliff Roberts had a perfectionist zeal and that he thought about the club "morning, noon, and night." Although the term obsessive-compulsive disorder was first used in 1903, it wasn't classified as a separate clinical diagnosis until 1980. Some highly accomplished innovators were obsessive-compulsive.

Nikola Tesla, the inventor of alternating current power systems, was obsessed with the number three. When he swam in a pool, he swam thirty-three laps; he would circle a city block three times before entering a building located on it; and he would only stay in hotel rooms whose number was divisible by three.

Howard Hughes had an obsession with germs and would wash his hands compulsively.

Neither Hughes nor Tesla was ever diagnosed with OCD, but they surely suffered from it.

Roberts made the golf shop at Augusta National give change in brand-new bills because he detested dirty bills (the golf shop still does this). He also organized all the cash in his pocket by denomination, with plenty of each bill on hand, to avoid receiving dirty bills in return as change. All the pictures hanging in the club had to be hung by two hooks because it irritated him if they were crooked. Roberts had maple and oak trees cut down from Augusta National because the falling leaves bothered him and made the course less immaculate. A good example that shows the degree to which Roberts was a stickler for detail beyond all reason comes from Ken Bowden, who collaborated with Roberts on his book. Bowden was once summoned to Augusta by Roberts; the fastidious chairman wanted to review the placement of six punctuation marks. Roberts was never diagnosed with OCD, and the reader can draw their own conclusion about whether he had the disorder—or whether he was just an eccentric about details.

When Steve Jobs was a young boy, he helped his father build a fence in their yard. Walter Isaacson, author of a bestselling biography of Jobs, wrote that he learned a lifelong lesson from the experience: "A true craftsman uses a good piece of wood even for the back of a cabinet against the wall, his father explained, and they should do the same for the back of the fence. It was the mark of an artist to have such a passion for perfection."

Whether we call the behaviors of Jobs, Roberts, Hughes, and Tesla personality quirks or something else isn't the point; it's that they achieved great things through their pursuit of perfection.

I toyed with naming this chapter "Perfectionism," rather than "Focus on the Details," but being perfect is not an action you can take—it is the result of a maniacal attention to detail. It is one of the factors that makes the Masters such a joy.

Professional golfers have as much awe for what Augusta National does as the rest of us. Below are some sentiments expressed by tournament participants.

> Scottie Scheffler: "I just think that their attention to detail is unmatched."

> Keegan Bradley: "It's probably the most attention to detail of anyplace in the world."

> Rickie Fowler: "There's really nothing that isn't done with a purpose."

The attention to detail begins with the language that is permitted and not permitted. The Masters has gallery guards and not marshals. Before play begins, the guards are instructed to remain on only one side of the hole they are working, to keep the course in the best possible condition. And one of their jobs is ensuring that the green Masters chairs patrons put down remain OCD straight and in alignment. The use of the word patron instead of fan or spectator seems trivial; you could argue it is a difference without a distinction, but there *is* an important difference. We most frequently use the word patron with the word arts: "She is a patron of the arts," and the terminology was born from the early days of the tournament when they had difficulty getting people to attend, and therefore they truly appreciated anyone who "patronized" the tournament.

The Masters does have more rules than most tournaments, including a no cell phone rule and a no running rule. No coolers are allowed, and bringing in a flag, a sign, or a banner is verboten. No strollers are allowed, and except during practice rounds, no cameras are permitted. CBS camera operators following players are instructed to move into the trees, or out of the line of sight when they are not actively filming a shot, so that the overall aesthetic of the course is maintained, with less clutter.

No detail is too small to escape the tournament's notice. Two-time Masters winner Scottie Scheffler talks about how he noticed that the kitchen cuts the ring that seals new ketchup bottles before they come out, alleviating the need for the highly paid athletes to struggle with pulling off the annoying seals before they enjoy a burger. Details in the Champions Locker Room are also thought out to the minutest detail—the entry door has an Augusta National logo carved in the wood, the felt on the card tables is wiped to create a uniform appearance, and the pencils are laid out just so.

Every room in the large clubhouse looks new, recently renovated, and freshly painted. For those who dine inside the clubhouse, the pats of butter have an Augusta National logo pressed into them. The metal tabletops in the concession areas have logos cut into them, which isn't necessary or functional but adds a touch of class. The long dining table at the Champions Dinner to celebrate Jon Rahm's victory had floral arrangements running down the middle with yellow and red flowers that matched the colors on the Spanish flag. Of course they did, because that's part of the Masters's special formula.

I have a friend and onetime boss who worked at McKinsey & Company, and when he was an associate there, he was assigned to a job at Augusta National. The club hired McKinsey to do an analysis of the course and the property, and to make recommendations on what should be relocated or hidden—in particular, the bathrooms, garbage cans, and concession areas—so that anything that wasn't perfect would not be seen on television, to keep the look of the property as flawless as possible. The *New York Times* claims that while the tournament is in progress, one maintenance employee is assigned to every quarter-acre of the property, which means there would be fourteen hundred workers scattered about; it seems like a large number, but given how spotless the property is, it's probably true.

The bathrooms are another area where the attention to detail is noticeable. The buildings are made of pine, which is an artful design because it helps to overpower the foul with the fragrant. And there are jovial attendants that keep the lines moving both inside the building and out. "Welcome to the men's room!" is not a greeting one hears at even the fanciest hotel or restaurant, but an earnest greeting at the Masters. In addition to ensuring you are in and out quickly, the attendants clean the stalls after *each* use.

Players get special treatment, as you would expect, including the use of a brand-new Mercedes SUV during the tournament. At most golf tournaments, players use portable restrooms that are visible, but at the Masters they are permanent structures and well hidden.

The club has embraced the same philosophy used by a groundbreaking architect of the twentieth century, Mies van der Rohe. Mies, as he was known, reached his heyday in the 1950s, and he was one of the founders of the International Style of architecture, defined by its elegant simplicity. His most famous design was the Seagram Building on Park

Avenue in New York, and his underlying design philosophy was simple: "God is in the details."

Part of the reason the Masters is often compared to Disney theme parks is because much of the inner workings are hidden from patrons. "Disney shuddered at the thought of a young parkgoer spotting Mickey Mouse taking a lunch break and shattering their trust in his creations," Marco Margaritoff, a New York-based writer who has researched Disney wrote. "In order not to reveal the man behind the curtain, Disney built the 'utilidor' system to hide the everyday lives of workers from parkgoers."

Disney's Magic Kingdom Park in Orlando has a nine-acre tunnel complex containing everything cast members need, including ATMs, dining halls, and changing areas. Disney hired a retired general from the Army Corps of Engineers to oversee the building of the complex using above-ground tunnels. Because of the swampy terrain the park was built on, the utility corridors couldn't be sunk underground. When guests walk into the park, unbeknownst to them, they walk fifteen feet above ground level on a gradual incline, never realizing the beehive of activity occurring under their feet. Similarly, at the Masters, much of what allows the environment to be uncluttered and pristine is the fact that the infrastructure is hidden—cables are buried, the microphones on tees are hidden, and food in the concession stands is restocked using a dumbwaiter fed from a staging area below. Merchandise sold in the golf shop is refilled via a subterranean system that includes four freight elevators and nineteen merchandise lifts.

One of the fascinating facts about Central Park in New York is how multiple levels, corridors, bridges, and tunnels are designed in a way that is imperceptible to anyone enjoying the park because they fit together seamlessly. Frederick Law Olmsted and Calvert Vaux designed the park in 1858 with three constituents in mind—providing walkways for pedestrians, roads for horse-drawn carriages, and bridle paths—separating them for safety reasons and to avoid congestion. The carriage drives are now used by motor vehicles, and visitors rarely discover the four heavily trafficked roads traversing the park because they are sunken and hidden from view. Augusta National has taken a similar approach over the last two decades, building infrastructure that allows various constituencies to travel around the property with minimal interactions.

Before 2016, when patrons walked from the parking lots toward the entry gates, they needed to wait for traffic before they could enter. It required sheriffs and security guards to orchestrate the movements. Always attuned to how they can make the experience just a little better each year, the club worked with the city of Augusta to reroute the road and put in two wide tunnels with fancy stonework walls to solve the problem. In 2020, the club built another tunnel 120 feet long under heavily-trafficked Washington Road to connect to their brand-new, forty-acre Global Broadcast Village.

There is also a tunnel to ferry players and members from the clubhouse to the media center; and there are roads around the perimeter of the course not visible to patrons that allow various service vehicles to do their business quietly. Their attention to detail is so advanced—with beautification a part of each design—that patrons hardly ever notice that something has changed, because the club manages their improvements with the same design philosophy that was achieved in Central Park. They are imperceptible and seamless.

The unsung heroes behind Augusta National's perfection are its greenkeepers and nursery crew, the latter a group of fifteen to twenty specialists who look after the trees, flowers, shrubs, and bushes. A motivational plaque that hangs in the club's maintenance facility describes their operating philosophy: "The difference between ordinary and extraordinary is that little extra."

The fact that it is impossible to find a weed or any imperfections on the property speaks to an unparalleled perfection. Pine Valley is the only other course I know of whose grassed areas are as pristine as those at Augusta National, and it is one of the reasons it is ranked as the number one course in the world. Augusta National has thirty-five greenkeepers, far more than most courses, and the number swells to well over one hundred during tournament week, with superintendents and greenkeepers from well-maintained clubs around the country asked to come in and assist. They trim bunker edges and other parts of the course by hand with scissors, creating a pristine look.

Each mower has a tennis ball dangling from a string in front of the driver so that if he or she notices a hydraulic leak on a mower in front of them, they remove their tennis ball and throw it in front of the mower with the leak to alert them to stop. Several years ago, a hydraulic leak occurred before play started on a competition day, and within fifteen minutes, they had already begun to replace the turf. Deep pockets have their benefits.

The grass along the steep banks of the ponds is cut using special lawnmowers attached to ropes that the crews pull up and down, since a conventional lawnmower or weed-whacker wouldn't reach. Not only is the sand at Augusta

National different from almost any other course, but the ponds contain food dye, making them a uniform and pleasing color. There has been speculation that the club puts ice on the azalea beds if the weather has been warm, to slow budding in an attempt to ensure peak bloom. The club denies it, as does a former greenkeeper, who said it would be impractical given the sheer number of them.

When the course is closed during the stifling heat of the summer, the greenkeepers don't get a break, continually nurturing the course, putting up protective shades over tees and greens, and installing large blower fans to promote air circulation. The yellow flower beds planted in logo patterns are maintained using a low-slung vertical ladder, so the workers can reach the middle of the six-foot beds without damaging other flowers. Technically, the nurserymen could reach in and weed or trim if they wanted, but they risk crushing a flower. It's just one more demonstration that shows how much each detail is thought through so as not to spoil the perfect environment.

Even the trees at Augusta National are manicured, with some deliberately cut to lean inwards, making the fairways appear narrower. The concept of manicuring trees is a rarity among golf courses in America. Most courses maintain trees simply to keep up the course's appearance, to ensure they don't become overgrown and impede play, and so they don't limit airflow, which is bad for the turf. What is different about Augusta National's approach is the degree of meticulousness they apply to it.

Their approach is similar to that of Hirono, a private club located near the port city of Kobe in Japan. Hirono has been dubbed the Pine Valley of Japan for its exclusivity, its degree of difficulty, and because of the exacting standards they have in place regarding maintenance. Their maintenance program isn't focused only on greens and fairways, but is much the same as Augusta National's; it extends to the entire property. When I played Hirono, there was a crew using cherry-pickers, carefully sculpting branches and limbs high up in the trees, manicuring them so they were pleasing to the eye. Our host mentioned that they are continually refining the trees, working on them like they are a Japanese garden. Which they are.

The attention to detail at Hirono is indicative of Japanese society generally. When I took the Shinkansen bullet train from Tokyo to Kobe, the train arrived at the exact minute it was supposed to. Not within a minute or two of its scheduled time, but precisely on time, and Japan Railways tracks delays to the second because it is a point of pride. Taxis also pay attention to detail, which is impressive—cabs in Japan are spotless, drivers wear white gloves, and the doors open automatically when you approach. The same attention is shown when checking into a hotel; multiple staff members at the front desk walk out from behind the counter and bow to greet you. Each detail in the room is thought out, down to the heated toilet seats in the bathrooms. Augusta National's approach mirrors the Japanese way.

If Augusta National didn't focus on seemingly unimportant details, then their golf course and tournament would not have the exalted status it has. I remember when I arrived at Augusta National on the day I was playing with 1998 Masters winner Mark O'Meara. As we walked to check in for the Masters, we went to two tournament buildings behind the scenes. Two sidewalks connected at an acute angle, leaving an irregular area between them about one foot by three feet in size. Within that small area was a patch of grass as perfectly manicured and trimmed as anything on the property. It was classic Steve Jobs back-of-the-fence mentality. It doesn't matter to the club that it won't be seen by patrons or on television—they still want it to be exquisite. That is focusing on the details.

## Lessons from Augusta National Members

"Pay attention to details. Getting the facts is key to good decision making. Every mistake I made came because I didn't take the time. I didn't drive hard enough." – Charles Knight, former chairman Emerson Electric

# How to Focus on the Details

The reason the perfection of the Masters stands out is because it is so rare to find. When we find an event or a brand that elevates itself, we find it admirable.

Millions of restaurants across the globe serve good food, but fewer than 3,000 have a Michelin star, denoting a level of excellence and an attention to detail that other restaurants haven't achieved. In the same way going to the Masters isn't just visiting a golf course, going to a Michelin-starred restaurant isn't just going for a meal. It is something special and typically no detail is overlooked, including the floral displays in the dining room, the quality of the wait staff, the care taken selecting the best wine glasses and dinnerware, and the exacting presentation of the food. Attention to detail sets the Michelin-starred apart, and the owners and staff have an elevated sense of pride, always striving to improve.

It's the same sense of pride a Parisian boulangerie or patisserie typically has, with an equally passionate focus and scrupulousness. Americans are usually dumbfounded when they first taste a freshly baked baguette or croissant in Paris. They taste so good because the baker-owner woke up at 3:00

a.m. and has been toiling over minor details for hours to make them as perfect as possible. Not that there aren't bakeries and bread shops in the U.S. that do the same, but it is much harder to find that same perfection that exists in France, which is why it is such a revelation when we taste it.

While the best restaurants and bakeries are determined to focus on the details, they are typically small operations with one location, making it easier to accomplish. What about companies or brands that offer their products and services to a wider audience? There are a handful that are superior to others and make the commitment, ruthlessly focusing on the details—Four Seasons, Lamborghini, Rolls-Royce, Chateau Lafite Rothschild, and Patek Philippe, to name a few. My favorite comparison, and the one that most closely aligns with the Masters, is Ritz-Carlton.

## Ritz-Carlton

Mirroring the Masters, Ritz-Carlton had a visionary founder, César Ritz. Ritz ingrained a focus on detail into the company, beginning with the first hotels he opened in Paris (the Ritz) and London (the Carlton). After Ritz's death, the company opened its first hotel in the U.S., in Boston, in 1927, retaining the same attention to detail, sometimes going to extravagant lengths to do so. If necessary, the hotel would redecorate entire rooms to suit specific guests. When Winston Churchill visited, they changed the upholstery in his room to red linen, his favorite color. César's son, Charles, was still pointing out quality improvements that could be made at the hotels until the week he died at age eighty-four.

One of the firms I worked for had a special deal with Ritz-Carlton, and I have stayed at their hotels many times while traveling on business. I never had a disappointing experience. Their attention to detail begins from the moment you enter the hotel. The lobbies are spotless, the music is low-key, and the lighting is subdued. All hotels use technology to manage their properties, but the technology at Ritz-Carlton is superior. Staff members are encouraged to put guest preferences into "preference pads," and then the information is shared with all their properties. This allowed them to get the details right, including my preferred room locations and my preferred newspaper. My wife is allergic to feather pillows, so they were changed to non-allergenic. Every time.

One of Ritz-Carlton's three steps of service is "Anticipate and fulfill each guest's needs." For years, I frequently visited their property in the French Quarter of New Orleans. Virtually every staff member remembered my name. When I came to breakfast, they remembered the table I preferred and how I took my coffee. Their focus on the details made all the difference, making me a loyal customer. My wife has a lot of food allergies, and when she traveled with me, the chef would come out of the kitchen to speak with her to understand exactly what she could and couldn't eat. That's focusing on the details.

Beyond attention to detail, Ritz-Carlton has developed a distinct language, which may seem contrived, but it does help create an elevated sense of purpose. Their motto is, "We are Ladies and Gentlemen serving Ladies and Gentlemen." Their service values incorporate principle number five and include an element of constant improvement: "Continuously seek opportunities to innovate and improve the Ritz-Carlton experience." Each employee is required to "continually" identify any defects at their properties so they can be fixed. Their values also include, "I am responsible for uncompromising levels of cleanliness," which extends to the bathrooms.

Ritz-Carlton goes above and beyond almost any company I know and embodies the sixth principle of treating customers with respect. I love the approach they take, empowering *any* employee at *any* level to spend $2,000 on a guest if needed. If a problem occurs and a guest is dissatisfied, any employee can fix it on the spot without needing approval from a manager. The former president of Ritz-Carlton, Horst Schulze, describes why they take this approach, comparing it to the standard of care a mother uses with a child. When a child has a problem, the mother doesn't say, "Let me call the manager." She fixes the problem. The company strives to do the same, and it's a pity more companies don't.

Many companies fear emulating Ritz-Carlton's approach because they think it will be abused and cost them dearly. The experience at Ritz-Carlton shows that it is not the case. Counterintuitively, it is rarely used. It does, however, change the dynamic of how guests are treated (with immense respect), and equally as important, it shows trust in employees, treating them as adults who can handle responsibility. Empowering employees is transformative. When a problem arises, there is a striking difference between a real person offering a sincere apology, as opposed to someone reading word-for-word from a script, "I. Am. Sorry. For. Your. Problem," when they obviously aren't.

Ritz-Carlton also aims to incorporate "mystique" into its brand, one of the rarest characteristics an organization can have. It is not a specific set of actions to take, but rather, it's about "reviving the emotions and memories of guests by genuinely caring and making them feel recognized, important, and unique." Appropriately enough, the customer-centric technology system Ritz-Carlton uses to provide such superior service is named "Mystique." The Masters also has an element of mystique, and the similarity of the two experiences is that it makes people feel great.

## Buc-ee's

All the brands I have referenced that exhibit a profound attention to detail are premium brands and require affluence to enjoy them, although affluence is not always necessary. I know it's odd to keep returning to bathrooms, but to me, it is the ultimate measure of whether an organization is focused on details or not. The bathrooms at the Masters are the perfect example—spotlessly clean. Would you believe a chain of travel centers located along highways can achieve a Masters level of success by focusing on the details? Buc-ee's, a privately held company based in Texas, makes cleanliness a part of their mission statement, and their website touts that they have the "cleanest restrooms in America!" Buc-ee's has fifty-eight locations in the South, all of which are open twenty-four hours a day, every day of the year. Their superstore in New Braunfels, Texas, has a Texas-sized eighty-three restrooms, with three shifts working to keep them clean around the clock.

Buc-ee's stores have a cult following, and motorists drive out of their way because they know the restrooms won't be filthy, as is common along busy highways. Buc-ee's doesn't have the resources Augusta National or Ritz-Carlton has, but they are committed to focusing on the details, which has helped them differentiate.

In *Forbes'* annual customer experience "All-Stars" list, compiled based on customer surveys, Buc-ee's ranked number one, above all other brands and companies. Their number one rank is not compared to other convenience stores or gas stations, but to *all* other brands. They receive Masters-like accolades:

"This is proof that the perfect place does exist."
"Epic."
"Warm friendly smiles, love the energy of the staff."

Their merchandising is also at a Masters level, with those stopping for gas typically spending more than fifteen minutes inside their stores (spending an hour or more is not uncommon), which are often the size of a Walmart, and filled with a crazy assortment of Buc-ee's branded gear.

### Lessons from Augusta National Members

"Many people regard execution as detail work that's beneath the dignity of a business leader. That is wrong. To the contrary, it's a leader's most important job. Organizations don't execute unless the right people, individually and collectively, focus on the right details at the right time." – Larry Bossidy, former CEO, Honeywell

# CHAPTER NINE

# Principle #3

# Don't Be Overly Commercial

IN the movie *A Christmas Story*, set in 1940, the main character, nine-year-old Ralphie, was excited to follow Little Orphan Annie in her serialized radio show, faithfully listening to hear clues. When he finally received his secret decoder pin in the mail, he barricaded himself in the bathroom to find out the secret message because "the fate of the planet may hang in the balance." To his shock and dismay, he discovered it was "a crummy commercial" for Ovaltine.

For every hour the Masters is on the air, only four minutes of commercials are shown. When NBC broadcasts the British Open, there are twenty frustrating minutes of commercials per hour—five times what the Masters shows. The same with the other majors, although sometimes they show mercy on the weary viewer, and the last hour is commercial-free, but by that point, so many brain cells have been killed that it's a Pyrrhic victory. Notably, the Masters has no advertisements on the course, the only professional sporting event that takes this approach.

In contrast, the Waste Management Phoenix Open plasters logos everywhere they conceivably can. Waste Management is paying good money to sponsor the tournament and increase their brand recognition, so they organize it to maximize the number of eyeballs seeing their logo. They place logos on the grandstands, the waste receptacles scattered around the course, and the pin flags. Fittingly, the tee markers are miniature garbage trucks with WM logos on them. The logos are even painted on the top of grandstands, so they get their money's worth when the blimp shoots aerial shots.

This is the opposite of what viewers of CBS's broadcast of the Masters see, the same for patrons who attend the tournament in person; both only see the greenery of the course and the beauty of the flora in bloom. One of the reasons the Masters is the most watched tournament of the year is because the broadcast is non-commercial and soothing to watch; it's noticeable what's not there.

The most illuminating way to understand how good—and rare—the Masters phenomenon is, is to look at what happens when commercialism runs amok. Watching a Major League Baseball game has become nightmarish because viewers are bombarded with new forms of advertising. I'll start by highlighting three. First, breaking with tradition, Major League Baseball recently made the pimpish decision to put advertisements on players' sleeves. Second—aside from a handful of historic venues such as Fenway Park and Dodger Stadium—the stadiums are advertisements: Loan Depot Park,

Comerica Park, Minute Maid Park, etc. Third, computer-generated ads are projected on the television screen behind the pitcher's mound and along the baselines.

MLB Network is the worst offender as an overly commercialized sports broadcaster. Their broadcasts have become Fellini movies: extravagant circuses. There is not even one second when an advertisement is not on the screen. Check that. Never. For fun, I recorded a random MLB Network broadcast: the Marlins versus the Giants. Stopwatch in hand, I watched for one hour, timing each commercial. On the surface, it technically isn't awful—thirteen minutes of commercials.

But.

That is just looking at traditional linear television commercials, i.e., the ones they show between innings or during pitching changes—technically it's no longer a pitching change, but a Florida Lottery call to the bullpen—when there is no action on the field. The screen had four chyron boxes throughout the game along the bottom. Each chyron had content and scrolling ads, including a Bally's logo on display continually in the middle of the four boxes.

Baseball stadium interiors are also laden with ads. I saw electronic billboard-style ads on the stadium walls for twelve brands, including Nathan's Famous, whose tagline on the digital display proudly announced, "It's all about the beef." It certainly is. It perfectly sums up the problem with MLB Network: too much filler, not enough beef. We want to watch baseball, not a brand bombardment. In the sixty minutes I watched, I saw what they call in the advertising business "impressions" of forty-seven brands, excluding duplicate ads. The Masters has only four television brand sponsors. In the movie *Amadeus*, the emperor famously critiques Mozart after sitting through a performance that he was overwhelmed with, saying, "There are in fact, only so many notes the ear can hear in the course of an evening . . . there are simply too many notes." And so it is with MLB Network. There are in fact, simply too many ads.

Growing up, I watched the Yankees on a local station, WPIX. We owned a large, bulky television filled with vacuum tubes. It had a fiddly rabbit ear antenna that had to be positioned just so to get a clear picture. There were only rudimentary graphics, and nowhere near the level of advertising that exists today. Pulling up clips of games from the late '70s and early '80s on YouTube, it is striking what wasn't seen: behind the plate is just blue padding, no ads. There are various reasons for the decline in baseball viewership, but the increased ad time has to be a factor.

The commercialism gets even worse. In an effort to make more money at the expense of fans, the Yankees have sold their broadcast rights to a half-dozen partners. A search engine and broadcast directory are needed to watch Yankees games now. I subscribe to the team-owned YES Network, but increasingly, games are broadcast on Amazon Prime Video, Apple TV+, Fox, and ESPN. And somehow, WPIX survived and still carries an occasional game, but I have no idea what cable channel they are affiliated with. The net result is the need to buy subscriptions totaling $1,425 for a collection of services to watch what was once free, and less commercially oriented.

It's sad what has happened to our Great American Pastime, yet most sports, including golf, seem to be going down the same path—"playing through" commercials began golf's downward spiral. Fingers crossed that the future doesn't hold ads projected onto fairways and greens, or scrolling electronic ads along the grandstands, or gambling odds on the screen *throughout* the broadcast.

I empathize with sports broadcasters; it is a tough business. In the last five years their business model has become a doom loop. The more ads they put on, the more viewers they lose, and then advertisers aren't willing to pay as much for their airtime. They then put *even* more ads on to make up the difference, and the spiral continues downward.

Cliff Roberts predicted the doom loop fifty years ago—his idea, as retold by David Owen, was that, "If Augusta National, the USGA and other tournament sponsors insisted on extracting every dollar they could, the time devoted to commercials would have to increase to cover the networks' inflated costs." Very prescient. This is exactly what happened. He also offered the solution: "The proper way to think of television, Roberts believed, was as a long-term investment rather than a short-term bonanza." Sadly, it's likely that the train has already left the station, and it would be difficult for current broadcasters to radically change their business models, with fans left to suffer the consequences.

The Internet has many parallels to the trends in broadcasting, with customers expressing a clear preference for a less commercially driven world. Masters.com is commercial-free, except for unobtrusive sponsor logos placed in non-prominent locations. It's what we expect from the Masters, and they don't let their loyal fan base down.

Like a frog being boiled, we have submitted little by little to the advertising barrage on websites. We willingly let Google track our browsing history and product preferences in exchange for a free search engine and email. The data is then sold to Facebook and others, who show as many ads as content as we scroll through their sites. Google Jimmy Dean sausage or Devil Dogs, and the next time you are reading the *Wall Street Journal* online, there it is. Your affinity for Devil Dogs has been noted, and the ads appear among the news. Or the next time you visit ESPN.com, they know you could be a sausage boy and serve up ads accordingly.

News websites are particularly bad. Foxnews.com is laden with ads, as is CNN.com. The organizations need to make enough money to pay the bills, so banner ads now take up *one-third* of the screen. The *Los Angeles Times* website is appalling; even paid subscribers are subjected to an abundance of ads that make it difficult to read the content. Sites such as the *Economist*, the *New Yorker*, and the *Atlantic* can be ad-free, but subscribing to their content is expensive.

"We are in a world where it will be increasingly possible to avoid ads," Brian Wieser of Madison and Wall, an advertising consulting firm, notes. He highlights a trend that mirrors the rest of society: a bifurcation between those with the wherewithal to pay and those without. YouTube offers a premium product allowing users to view their videos ad-free. It is wildly popular and has 100 million subscribers. Regulators forced Facebook to offer an ad-free product in Europe. Twitter (I don't do the "formerly-known-as" thing, and few people call it X anyway) also offers an ad-free premium option.

According to Marketing Dive, a firm that provides in-depth insights for marketers, more than half of surveyed U.S. consumers reported that overexposure to ads negatively impacted their perception of a brand. The study offers this additional insight: "When selecting an answer to the question 'which word best describes the ads you typically see…,' many consumers deemed advertising 'excessive' across television, social media, and the web." Data from various sources confirms we are becoming sick of the over-commercialization. Sixty-nine percent of people surveyed by Google said they installed ad blockers because of annoying or intrusive ads.

Amazon.com was once an attractive site filled with quality products and low prices. It had a simple search box, and its algorithm returned the best products. Now, the top section of their home page is a scrolling ad. The site has become so advertising-driven that it is losing its utility. Product searches now default to "featured" items, which is a euphemism for, "We're getting paid to show this product even if it's crap, because we receive revenue for doing so." Amazon touts its ad model to investors, who cheer the results. In 2023, Amazon made a whopping $31.6 billion in advertising revenue. That's more than McDonald's *total* revenue of $25.5 billion. The tech giant in Seattle has put investors first, at consumers' expense.

Monetization is a byword of our times, and virtually every product a website recommends receives affiliate commissions from Amazon or other retailers when you click the link to buy something. All those young ladies offering recipes online aren't necessarily doing so because they love cooking. They are earning affiliate commissions when you click. Read the fine print: "We may earn revenue from the products available on this page and participate in affiliate programs."

The same is true for blogs offering reviews of everything from garden hoses to new computers. They have an inherent conflict of interest in recommending products that fatten their wallets the most. A particularly successful practitioner is Peter Adeney, who runs a blog touting a frugal lifestyle; he makes over $400,000 a year in affiliate payments. "Influencers" on social media are paid to steer you into products they earn high affiliate commissions on, and some have become millionaires doing so. Enterprising individuals across the web who are seemingly offering advice or recommendations for free are often not.

Even as we pay to opt out of ads on television, radio, and the web, like a virus we can't shake, ads permeate spaces we can't control or opt out of. "A bone density test is recommended for women over sixty-five," an upbeat lady announces. I'm on the phone with Blue Cross and waiting for an agent. I'm already irritated because they denied my claim, and I must take time to call and get it resolved. I have been on hold for twenty minutes because the company prioritizes profitability ahead of serving clients. And I'm neither a woman nor over sixty-five. The indignity is far worse because I must listen to inane advertisements on a half-dozen topics while waiting. Not just once, but repeatedly, like a vinyl record whose needle has gotten stuck. I don't want to listen to this drivel; I want my problem solved quickly.

I worked for a credit card company for a decade, so I'm hardly in a position to criticize credit card marketing practices.

But.

The now common practice of being cross-sold card products while stuck in an airplane cabin has gone over the line. We can throw out the avalanche of junk mail that shows up in our mailboxes. We can turn our televisions off or change the channel if we don't want to watch commercials. But on a plane, we are captives. We all know the stress of getting through airport security, the stampede of the boarding process, and the indignity caused by the lack of personal space and ever-shrinking seats. I have flown United for decades and pay high prices for my tickets, but now, I am an object of marketing to boot. United does this because it is hugely lucrative. In 2023, they reported $2.7 billion in "other operating revenue" from partners, the bulk of which is from their co-branding agreement with Chase. They have a contractual obligation to market all the time: "United has a performance obligation to provide advertising in support of the MileagePlus card in various customer contact points such as United's website, email promotions, direct mail campaigns, airport advertising, and inflight advertising." The overly commercial model is one that the airlines have taken to heart because ferrying people from Louisville to Lubbock is a low-margin business.

Overbearing commercialism isn't a new pox on our society. The first advertisement in the Colonies appeared in 1704, in a Boston paper called the *News-Letter*. The first billboard in America appeared in 1835. The first television advertisement was in 1930, and the FCC fined the station that ran it because, at the time, advertising was not permitted. The first *legal* television ad ran in 1941, and it was a ten-second spot for Bulova watches that appeared, fittingly enough, during a baseball game. Even though advertising has been ingrained in our culture for over three hundred years, the level of commercialism has increased because new categories of ads have sprung up: ads while we are on hold, ads while we sit on planes, ads when we scroll through our phones, and ads when we visit websites. Even video ads on gas pumps.

Some of the biggest companies in our country—Google, Amazon, and Facebook—aren't technology companies per se; they are advertising companies that make hundreds of billions of dollars advertising to us. Because we spend so much time online, overall ad impressions *have* increased significantly. It's not only the number of ways that ads are delivered that has increased, but the frequency has also increased. As if those two factors weren't enough, new types of advertisers have also been added over the last fifty years, and we have to ask: were we better off or worse off with each new type?

Were we a better country when lawyers couldn't advertise? Spare me another highway billboard sign from an ambulance chaser. During a recent drive up the Eastern Seaboard, I saw scores and scores of them. Two that were memorable (for the wrong reasons): "Don't Scream, Call Akim," and "TopDog gets you top dollar." They are distasteful across the board, and practicing law was a more dignified profession before advertising.

Were we a better country before drug companies were granted the right to advertise on television? What idealized, sanitized, and fantasized parallel universe are drug commercials made in? They are universally bad, and it makes no sense. Only doctors can prescribe medicines, so who exactly are they targeted towards? And we end up paying more for drugs because the drug makers pass along the cost of their glitzy ads.

Were we a better country when there wasn't a fusillade of ads for online gambling? Lots of cleavage and celebratory dancing from the winners. The vice has become a virtue. The formula must be a lure for the unwitting, or they wouldn't keep doing it. Often, this doesn't end well (see Phil Mickelson).

Stephen Fox, author of an authoritative book about how the advertising business has evolved in our country, wrote forty years ago, "Advertising interrupts radio and television programs, crowds editorial matter off the pages of newspapers and magazines, disfigures city streets, defaces the countryside. Nobody believes it. It usually appeals to the less agreeable aspects of human nature: greed, vanity, insecurity, competitiveness, materialism." The title of his book is *The Mirror Makers*, which he chose because, "advertising acts like a mirror that merely reflects society back on itself." Which means that the mirror is telling us we have become a society of pill-popping, litigious gamblers who drive pickup trucks, buy a lot of insurance, and use credit cards freely.

The reason the Masters resonates both in person and on television is because it is an oasis, a respite from the boundless desert of commercialism we are trapped in. A shining example of how far the Masters takes their non-commercial approach can be seen in the guidelines they give to patrons using the new Map & Flag hospitality venue, where they ask them to be as commercial-free as possible, "Guests are asked to refrain from using any corporate signage, outerwear or company-specific lanyards. Guests are encouraged to use the Club-provided or Masters branded lanyards," to display their badges.

The world doesn't have to be as bad as it has become. Companies and sports organizations choose how commercial and money-oriented they want to be. Most have chosen to be highly commercial, which is a turn-off to customers. "It's a sad day when owners and commissioners choose money over the fans," was the reaction of Hall of Fame legend Charles Barkley when the NBA signed a television deal with a consortium that included the deep-pocketed Amazon Prime Video, which outbid the incumbent TNT. (One of the reasons I dislike Prime Video is because you can't flip back and forth between channels when commercials come on, like you can on cable. I'm not a fan of being force-fed.) Finishing the sentiment in eloquent words that were carefully selected, Barkley added, "It sucks."

We have a right to be angry and frustrated. It's not our imaginations; the level of advertising has increased, and has made watching television and using the internet very annoying. And, empirically, it *is* getting worse.

When asked in 1988 about the increasingly significant role money and sponsors were playing in professional golf, Augusta National chairman Hardin said the club would rather shut the tournament down than cave into commercialism. "I just don't believe the members of this club would want to continue if the only alternative was to get as much out of television as we could or to sandbag our patrons for every nickel, or to have hospitality houses all over the place."

It's nice to have one bulwark holding back the mercenaries.

### Lessons from Augusta National Members

"I don't visualize us having the Pizza Hut Masters." — Hord Hardin, former chairman Augusta National

# CHAPTER TEN

# How to Not Be Overly Commercial

Like the Masters, not all companies are overly commercial. Of special note are two of the most successful retailers of the last fifty years.

## Zara

The Spanish fast fashion retailer Zara takes an unorthodox approach to advertising. They don't do it. The market research firm SwiftERM explains their philosophy: "Zara does not advertise conventionally. You will not see a single television commercial, an ad in the press, a billboard, or banners on the Internet. Zara's marketing and advertising strategy is based on a concept that has been lost in the wake of the rise of new technologies and online stores. One of the most effective ways to get customers is to have them pass in front of your store, enter, and then buy." Zara pays premium rents to secure prime real estate, and that brings more people past their stores, and has proven effective in helping the company sell its products.

The firm also excels at using technology in a customer-focused manner. *Forbes* calls the augmented reality feature on their app "digital honey" because it helps to draw millennials into their stores. Scanning the QR code of an outfit brings a virtual model to life on the users phone, animating the experience and showing how fashionable the item looks.

Zara's non-commercial approach has made the company the world's largest fashion retailer, and its founder, Amancio Ortega, is the world's thirteenth wealthiest person.

## Costco

Try to recall the last time you saw an advertisement for Costco. How about never? James Sinegal, a co-founder and former CEO, explained the company's business model to the *New York Times*: "Sell a limited number of items, keep costs down, rely on high volume, pay workers well, have customers buy memberships and aim for upscale shoppers—especially small-business owners. In addition, don't advertise—that saves 2 percent a year in costs." Sinegal is a purist. He has even called advertising "evil."

Beyond not advertising, I was surprised to find that Costco did many things in the same vein as the Masters. The deeper I dug into their business philosophy, the more positive things I found. Costco has sold hot dogs for $1.50 for the last forty-seven years (it's actually a hot dog and drink combo with refills). They respect customers by not gouging and by allowing exchanges and returns without a receipt or time limit. And their stores are free of vexing music.

Ask an employee at any store, as I did several times, how it is to work there. They rave about the culture, how well they are paid, and the benefits. Employee turnover is less than 6 percent, orders of magnitude below those of other retail companies. They are famous for promoting from within, rewarding employees who have committed to the organization. Costco is also a proponent of the first principle and shows restraint regarding its growth strategy. Their expansion is limited by the pipeline of talent it nurtures in-house. Rather than expand faster, they intentionally slow their growth and won't open a new store until they have homegrown talent they can put in. Costco shows restraint in a world where the prevailing wisdom is growth at all costs.

Costco is a super successful company ranked by any metric. They are the third-largest retailer in the country behind Walmart and Amazon, and they rank fifth on the *Forbes* Customer All-Stars experience survey. Since going public in 1985, the stock has performed thirty times better than the stocks in the S&P 500 index, making it one of the best investments of the last forty years. All without advertising. Word of mouth is their most powerful generator of new customers.

In-N-Out Burger also takes a minimalist approach to commercialism. Lynsi Snyder highlights her firm's approach: "You'll hear a few radio commercials here and there. Every so often you'll hear a television commercial. Mostly we rely on word of mouth." In a world awash in commercialism, the Masters, Costco, In-N-Out, and Zara show that pursuing the opposite strategy can yield outsized results. Less is more.

No doubt, almost everyone looked at the contrast between what the Masters does and the way MLB Network operates and came to the same conclusion I did. Being less commercial is better. It is easy to be critical of big organizations, but the same analog can be applied to our personal lives. The enabler is often social media, which can become addictive. To a large degree, when people post their airbrushed lives on social media, they are advertising their own brand, often to create envy in others: "Look at me. I'm vacationing in Maui. And you're not." There's nothing wrong with that, but it's wise to step back and reflect from time to time. Am I limiting my commercial time like the Masters, or have I become an ad machine, cranking out self-promotion and chest thumping around the clock? All the world's a stage—even more so with Instagram, TikTok, and Facebook—but we don't have to be in performance mode constantly. Posting on social media is like consuming alcohol. Best done in moderation.

# CHAPTER ELEVEN

# Principle #4

# Use Technology Wisely

The best technologists are in their twenties and wear hoodies and sneakers.

Or so the prevailing wisdom goes.

Yet, a committee of five well-heeled Augusta National members, whose average age is sixty-six, have created a technology strategy that stands up against the best in the world. The five rule breakers who constitute the Digital Technology Committee for the Masters are:

- Brian L. Roberts, chairman & CEO of Comcast
- Hugh L. McColl III, partner at Collwick Capital, LLC
- Timothy P. Neher, cable television executive
- Samuel J. Palmisano, former CEO of IBM
- Brady L. Rackley III, technology entrepreneur

To be fair, these aren't five random AARP members on Social Security. Rackley and McColl are sophisticated entrepreneurs and investors, and Roberts, Neher, and Palmisano know a thing or two about technology and broadcasting. A commonality shared with other principles, the club's approach to technology is exemplary because it is restrained and non-commercial. The club has a superior story to tell, and new technologies have allowed them to craft it in a way that enables them to reach new audiences. As we saw in the second chapter with their multi-platform approach introducing and marketing the gnome, their ability to evolve and adapt has become a hallmark of an organization rich with tradition.

We live in an age where advances in technology are so rapid and innovative, it can be difficult to put into context what was at one time considered a new technology over the last one hundred years or so. Electricity, telephones, automobiles, air conditioners, washing machines, and radios were once all the latest technologies. The Masters was an early adopter of several new technologies through the decades, beginning with the first tournament. Telephones were installed near each green to report scores more quickly, and as soon as scores were available, they were relayed to a scoring control room. Once in the control room, they were transmitted by Telautograph—an early and crude precursor of a fax machine—to the press building. The tournament was an early adopter of walkie-talkies when it was a new technology.

It would be decades before the club would really harness new technologies to improve the tournament and the fan experience, but a focus on continually trying and adapting to them has always been a philosophy used at the club.

The Masters technology strategy spans fifteen different social media platforms, with content customized to match the vibe and norms of each. Here is a smattering of comments from the Masters Instagram account:

> "Greatest social media team in history."
> "Content is unreal. Perfect cinema."
> "This is the best Instagram account content. Period. The overall photography and cinematography is second to none. The best of the best."
> "An aesthetic dream."
> "Details. All in the details."
> "Who has been making all this content … because they have been producing absolute magic."

Despite producing such compelling content, the Masters has been quiet about their broad use of social media. They almost seem afraid to trumpet how good they are because it might upset traditionalists. So far—like almost everything they do—they have threaded the needle perfectly, balancing tradition with innovation.

At the end of each tournament day the club posts "goodnight" videos on Instagram that are especially notable, taking full advantage of the light during the golden hour—the yellow pansy flowerbed logo on Founders Circle shot in the foreground, contrasting with the soft glow of the light from the clubhouse in the background; time lapsed images of a lingering twilight over the thirteenth green, with long shadows dancing around; a pink and gray full moon centered in a fading blue sky over a leaderboard. Images taken in the early morning are equally good—the rising sun peeking through the pines; multicolor flower beds leading the eye to a Masters logo on a pairing sheet box; Augusta National members in their green jackets out among the dew, determining pin placements.

When the account launched in 2014, the content creators bumbled around initially. Despite the weak start, they found their footing the following year. Their artistic Instagram account has almost 2 million followers, making it their most popular social media platform.

The club has a reputation for being guarded; like the Vatican, it prefers to keep details about its inner workings close to the vest. Although they don't allow the media to cover certain aspects of the club and the tournament, their Instagram account reveals more— players registering for the tournament, detailed photos of the Champions Dinner, action of the greenkeepers doing their magic, and the piece-de-résistance, a red-shirted Tiger being fitted for his green jacket in the Champions Locker Room after his 2019 victory.

The Masters definition of growing the game is broad; as such, they also have an Instagram account in Japanese. Unsurprisingly, the content focuses on the Japanese players in the field. A custom menu written in Japanese for Hideki Matsuyama and posted on the site highlights the club's never-ending focus on getting all the little details right. There is also a separate Instagram account in Spanish, emphasizing Hispanic golfers. The Spanish and Japanese accounts also have unique and funny gnome videos.

For years, I sat in fancy conference rooms in Midtown Manhattan and listened to consultants from McKinsey & Company and Bain & Company as they flipped through glossy presentations, throwing out buzzwords. "First-mover advantage" was a big one. The theory is that the sooner an organization brings a product to market, the better. Being first gives a compelling advantage, particularly as it relates to technology.

That's the theory.

In practice, it rarely works.

Pets.com was a first-mover, launching in 1998 and closing its doors in 2000.

Netscape Navigator was an early web browser that no longer exists.

The spreadsheet Lotus 1-2-3 was one of the killer apps on early IBM personal computers; Apple's version was VisiCalc, launched in 1979 on the Apple II. Microsoft's Excel now dominates the spreadsheet market.

Sony launched its Betamax VCR system before the rival VHS system, but the latter entrant overtook it.

Myspace was the first social network to reach scale but was subsequently crushed by Facebook.

Not only does the Masters break the first-mover advantage rule, but they also go against the grain in their implementation approach. The engineering work is not done by a technology company in Palo Alto or San Jose, but by one founded in 1911 in Endicott, New York—the old-school and stodgy IBM. In the '70s and '80s IBM's male employees were clones, known for their strict adherence to the company dress code—white button-down shirts, dark suits, wing-tip shoes, and a notable absence of facial hair. Big Blue is now getting her revenge on the West Coast tech darlings, outshining them all with her superior creations—Masters.com and the polished Masters app. Axios calls their app the best in sports, and one could make a case for it being one of the best outside of sports, too. It rises above with its clean aesthetic, ease of navigation, and inventive content.

The club has reached into the bottom of its deep pockets to fund such brilliance. Augusta National doesn't do mediocre. Since the 1970s, the chairman of IBM has traditionally been invited to join Augusta National, so to say they had an inside track to win the Masters mandate understates the case. We don't know the process IBM uses to choose which employees get the plum assignment to work on the Masters project, but we can have confidence they are not choosing B players to code and design what has become their showcase.

The company's website uses it to tout their sophistication and prowess, especially in their use of artificial intelligence (AI). "IBM uses watsonx to manage the entire lifecycle of generative AI models that instantly reveal the risks and rewards for every shot on every hole at the Masters. The moment a shot comes to rest, the x, y, and z coordinates are captured, compared against years of historical data, and a Hole Insight is generated in the Masters app. More than 20,000 video clips in the Masters app are narrated —in both English and Spanish—by a generative AI model that's trained to speak the specific language of this tournament."

The Masters approach to technology is dissimilar to the agile approach in favor among techies today; it has more parallels to how the Japanese approach product development—waiting, assessing, and then adapting. While American auto makers struggled with quality issues in the late '70s and '80s, the Japanese focused on consistency and the smallest details. Although not first to market, the quality of their products led to their rise as one of the dominant automobile manufacturing countries. *Front Office Sports* asked an executive at IBM what it's like to partner with the Masters. "They're probably one of the more progressive partners in terms of experimentation," Noah Syken, the vice president of sports and entertainment for the company said, "but they're probably also one of the more conservative partners in terms of rolling things out to production."

Twitter is their second most popular social media platform, with 1.6 million followers spread across accounts in English, Spanish, and Japanese. The accounts are playful—one popular post animates a Lego Tiger Woods holing out a putt. Because the Masters Twitter account posts non-controversial content and doesn't respond to comments, it has escaped the negativity generally associated with the platform. Facebook is their third most popular social media platform, with 1.5 million followers. The content is good, but not nearly as compelling as the content on Instagram, primarily because Facebook has a more cluttered layout since it is not an image-and-video-first platform.

The Masters TikTok account has 1.2 million followers, and like Instagram, it *is* particularly well suited to video content. The account launched in 2022 with a video of the abstract expressionist artist Zach Frank using his signature dabbing technique to paint the Masters logo on a giant white canvas using soft squeeze plastic bottles filled with thick yellow, red, and green acrylic paint . . . with Verne Lundquist's "OH WOW!" call as the soundtrack. It's brilliant.

An especially creative video on their TikTok account is titled "The Tiger Effect." Using time-lapse photography, it is shot from the point of view of a patron standing behind the eighteenth tee, condensing down thirty minutes of action to a video of less than a minute, showing how a sparsely populated tee box swells over time to a crowd ten deep to watch Woods launch his ball in the air, and then the crowd ebbs again to just a handful of people when he leaves.

The most popular video posted is both surprising and not surprising. Consistent with the short attention spans of TikTok users, it is a twelve-second video of Bryson DeChambeau taken during the Par 3 Contest. After dunking his tee shot into the pond, he tees up again and flies the ball into the hole. He then points his index finger to the sky and says, "Thank you brother." It received 17 million views, 7 million more than watched the final round on television that year.

Declining golf television viewership was an inevitable part of the post-Tiger era. Some look at the trends and sound alarm bells. They may be looking at the wrong metric. Growing the game starts with engaging people who are new to golf. The Masters approach, working across a variety of channels and technologies, appears to be working. Samantha Marks, a former collegiate and professional golfer who posts on TikTok, has seen a shift in the online popularity of the Masters. "There were a lot more people, and specifically a lot more women and younger girls, talking about it," she said. "As somebody who played golf, loves the game, and is so deeply involved with it, that's really exciting to me."

The tournament's YouTube channel has almost six hundred thousand subscribers, and the content largely follows that of Masters.com, although they also have content in Japanese, Korean, and Spanish, and an Indian narrator speaking English, but with commentary tailored for those in India.

Millions of companies produce good content on social media; what is different about what the Masters is doing? Excluding celebrity accounts, there are other organizations that take the same approach as the Masters—National Geographic has one of the largest accounts on Instagram with almost 300 million followers, GoPro's account it also highly-rated, with spine-tingling point of view action videos; and NASA's account, spotlighting high-resolution images of space and the planets, shines. The common element of all four accounts is their combination of restraint, compelling imagery, and their non-commercial focus. When looked at from a consumer point of view, the answer on how a company should use social media is blindingly obvious—we want to laugh, we want to be entertained, we want to be awed, and we want to be inspired. That helps build the brand and elevates the unremarkable to the unforgettable. We don't want crummy commercials, which is sadly the way most organizations approach it.

The Masters launched its first website in 1996, using the URL masters.org. The user interface was rudimentary for the first decade. It wasn't until 2006 that the site started to have some of the look and feel it does today, and it was the first time "Amen Corner Live" was provided, offering twenty-two hours of coverage across all four tournament days, and it was transformative.

The man behind the pioneering changes bringing the tournament into the twenty-first century was someone former Atlanta mayor Andrew Young called, "an old-school Southerner," and he typified the term. Hootie Johnson was born in Augusta in 1931 and made his mark as the president of a small-town bank in South Carolina. The pugnacious, old-school Southerner wasn't a first-mover by any means, but he had a vision for how to use technology in the best fashion, understanding that not all technology advances have to be adopted immediately. And he understood the value in being selective. When the new capabilities were announced, Johnson said, "The importance and use of the Internet continues to grow, and we think this is another service to our patrons. The ability to see live action at Amen Corner is something very special."

Many French take August off to go on holiday, and the Spanish love an afternoon siesta. The golfer's equivalent begins the day the Masters starts. The addition of Amen Corner Live to the site instigated the biggest productivity waster into the work environment since the invention of the conference call, with golf lovers spending Thursday and Friday of the tournament glued to their work computers.

Additional productivity killers were added in the late 2010s. Final-round broadcasts of tournaments since 1968 were added to both their website and their YouTube channel, and video of every shot on every hole was made available using 110 state-of-the-art cameras (20,000 shots in total every year). To the consternation of cable companies across the country, the Masters website has made cutting the cord ever so easy. The club's philosophy of continuous improvement (principle five) has had the most profound impact on the Masters website and app, to a greater degree than on other parts of the tournament or television broadcast. As chairman Billy Payne said when launching a new set of features, "Trying to get better is simply a part of who we are at the Masters." Viewers can now pick and choose what to watch. The way each of the features was implemented is nearly flawless. Although he works for CBS's rival NBC, fourteen-time Emmy Award winner Jimmy Roberts serves as the voice of the Masters Digital, posting thoughtful and pitch-perfect videos throughout the week.

The streaming broadcasts on the website and app also follow the same standards set by the CBS broadcast, punctuating their thoughtful commentary with long periods of silence. The website draws 20 million viewers during the tournament. The "Round in Three Minutes" is popular in today's world of short attention spans, summarizing rounds of favorite players in the allotted time, showing only the key shots of the day.

Cliff Roberts said in *The Story of Augusta National,* "We are especially anxious to have the telecasts done in a first-rate fashion." If he were alive today and could see the telecasts produced on the website and the app, his anxiety would ease. And he finally got his wish. The streaming broadcasts have no commercial interruptions.

The Masters podcast launched in 2019 and is hosted by a real stylist—a spiky-haired, snappy dresser with a penchant for wearing loud jackets and colorful socks. Marty Smith is an ESPN reporter who covers a variety of sports for the network. Although he wouldn't seem a natural choice to host, his authenticity is complemented by an appealing Appalachian twang. Marty may be the most enthusiastic proponent of all things Augusta National and speaks about the fellowship that the tournament creates and how being on the grounds is a spiritual experience.

In addition to getting preferential access to champions past and present, his guest choices are eclectic and range from NASCAR drivers to NFL quarterbacks to the commissioner of the SEC football conference. The barrier to entry is low in the podcast world, with hundreds of golf podcasts available, but the Masters podcast is differentiated because Smith lets his guests talk for long periods without interrupting, and it benefits from the absence of advertisers.

Sometimes even the Masters creates duds. Their Snapchat account was established in 2022 to target the Gen Z and millennial demographics, although it has only a smattering of posts each year and appears to be flatlining. Their Pinterest account has a paltry fourteen hundred followers. The posts on the site appropriately have a home decorating feel, but are underwhelming. The Masters was an innovator in launching both 3D and 4D live streaming, but there was a lot stacked against the formats. Such is the innovator's life—some experiments work and others don't.

The SubAir system is another technology closely associated with Augusta National. The club installed the system under greens and crosswalks, and it has been a big success, providing a safer environment for patrons, and permitting the tournament to optimize green conditions.

Chairman Ridley says one of the things he thinks most about is striking the right balance between using technology smartly and respecting the tournament traditions. It is a tricky balancing act. When asked about how they surprised a lot of people—who never thought there would come a day when a drone would fly down Magnolia Lane, into the clubhouse, and out the Crow's Nest window, Ridley said, "We are not afraid to try things from time to time. I think we will continue to use creativity and digital while at the same time try to be true to our mission and who we are and remember those things that Mr. Roberts and Mr. Jones had in mind when they created the club, but it is not always easy."

Between the broadcasts, website, podcasts, social media sites, and the app, the Masters now generates more content than even the most enthusiastic fan can consume during tournament week, making the best week of the year even better. Using technology wisely means using it with restraint, without a commercial emphasis, and in a way that enriches people's lives. The Masters has struck the right balance, using technology in the wisest way.

### Lessons from Augusta National Members

"We don't perceive ourselves as being slow. We don't get carried away with new ideas." – John Weinberg, former chairman, Goldman Sachs

# CHAPTER TWELVE

# How to Use Technology Wisely

Technology can be used in two ways. To entertain, inform, and make our lives better and easier. Or to put roadblocks in place, or to serve a company's goal of lowering costs. It is easy to become myopically focused on the iPhone, convenience apps, and websites, and overlook the spectacularly good technology all around us. It's convenient that we can have a pizza delivered via DoorDash, but pause for a moment and think about advanced airbags, artificial hip joints, mRNA technology, advances in precision medicine, emergency generators, advanced weather radar that lets planes fly around thunderstorms, ATMs, and countless other innovations that unquestionably improve our lives. Or look at the Third World, and how technology advances in water filtration have saved countless lives.

Using technology the wrong way creates negative experiences and wastes our time. We've all had the frustrating experience trying to get through call trees that are designed to put us off and dissuade us from speaking to a competent person. Or technology that facilitates the movement of call centers overseas. The worst examples are putting in idiotic bots that can't answer even the simplest questions. Or forcing us to look at frequently asked questions online instead of allowing us to call or email a company for help. As if those aren't bad enough, when we seek help, companies are increasingly pushing us to their online forums, Twitter discussions, or Reddit discussions (please!), instead of providing a way for us to interact with a human who can help.

All the aforementioned methods assume that the customer is a moron or won't get mad enough to find another provider.

Yes, we know we can pay our bill or check an account balance online, so don't insult us with simpleton answers that tell us how to do the basics. We're searching for help because we have a *complex* problem that can't be easily solved. The Masters is the North Star of implementing technology intelligently, using it to provide information in an uncluttered environment, and to entertain via their social media, videos, and podcasts. There are other companies that also use technology to help, rather than to dissuade or cut costs, including a little-known company located in the heartland.

## Uline

Unlike the examples focused on terrible service, the opposite end of the spectrum is a privately held company, Uline, based in Pleasant Prairie, Wisconsin. Uline sells cardboard boxes, packaging materials, bubble wrap, and other office supplies. Whenever I call Uline, they pick up the phone immediately. Often, I don't even hear the phone ring. Uline's phone support is open twenty-four hours a day, seven days a week, 365 days a year. A testimonial from their website reads,

"Knowledgeable representatives. I think you know what I want to order before I do." I have had the same experience; before I finish my sentences, they know what product I want to order based on their excellent technology and my past order history. Even when ordering multiple products at a time, it is rare that I am on the phone with Uline for more than three minutes from beginning to end because they respect my time. "We answer the phones faster than 911," Angelo Ventrone, vice president of logistics at the company, says. "And you will get a rep on the phone that is well-trained and familiar with our products." My experience exactly.

Uline's website is equally impressive. It is fast, uncluttered, non-commercial, and easy to use. I can accomplish what I set out to do in a minimal amount of time without frustration or a half-dozen solicitations for new products. If a smallish company in Wisconsin can provide this level of service, why can't our largest banks, insurance companies, package delivery companies, and utilities? Because they choose not to and want to save money instead. They are intentionally and blissfully oblivious to what their customers want. It's the very definition of being penny-wise, pound-foolish.

## Ikea

Ikea is another company that uses technology in a helpful and uncluttered manner. Beyond being helpful, it is also fun to use. They offer augmented reality on their app and website, which they call Kreativ. A room in your house can be easily scanned in three dimensions using your phone. You then get to pick and choose furniture and accessories that appear in the virtual room. Alternatively, users can pick blank rooms and furnish them visually to understand what works and what doesn't. The tool is inspirational and allows for creativity and idea generation. Unlike some firms that over-engineer their products, assuming we're MIT engineers, the Ikea tool is intuitive, allowing users to jump right into what matters. Items appear or disappear when you click, as if by magic. The chief digital officer for the company uses all the requisite techie jargon in describing how they achieve such a fantastic experience for customers: "These include AI neural networks which have been specially trained to recognize the objects and geometry of indoor spaces, stereo vision algorithms to see in 3D, computational photography algorithms to provide expansive photography, and mixed reality 3D graphics for realism." Translation for non-techies: "It's very cool." The other smart part of their technology design is that it isn't pushy. No pop-up boxes are cluttering it up with coupons or offers. And, no advertisements.

## Capital One

One of the latest buzzwords in the investment world is fintech (a portmanteau of financial + technology)—disruptive start-ups focused on the financial world. *Fintech Nexus News* called Capital One "the original fintech," growing from a startup to one of the ten largest banks in the country in thirty years. The primary reason for that success is Rich Fairbank, the seventy-three-year-old co-founder and CEO. Rich has an insatiable appetite to learn and has continually reoriented the firm to be tech-first. Ahead of his time, he founded the company in 1994, before PayPal, Google, and Facebook existed, on an "information-based strategy." Detail-oriented beyond anything you can imagine, Rich loves a good

PowerPoint presentation chock-full of data as a way to learn about new technology. When I worked at Capital One it wasn't uncommon for Rich to spend half a day going through a hundred-page presentation given by associates in their twenties, educating him in detail on the latest technologies.

Most CEOs would rarely, if ever, have contact with someone six or seven levels down in their organization, but given Rich's insatiable appetite to keep up with technology, he did it all the time. He has spent tens of billions of dollars ensuring Capital One remains on the leading edge of technology. It's quite an accomplishment for a septuagenarian, and it mirrors the approach taken by the "more experienced" group on the Digital Technology Committee at the Masters. (The preferred term for people who are older is now "more experienced," I've been told.)

One nugget we can take away from the Masters's technology approach, especially for those who are more experienced, is that in a world awash in technology, there is benefit in embracing it. It can be counterintuitive for those set in their ways. Why bother to find out what TikTok or Roblox are all about? Or why look at the latest tech gadget? Because once we stop being inquisitive, we go backwards. Having a mindset of continually learning, especially learning and embracing new technologies, can be quite enriching. If the buttoned-up members of Augusta National can use the latest technologies wisely, it's a lesson we can all learn from. For those with "less experience" (it's not kosher to call people young or younger anymore, even though they are), one takeaway is not to fall for all the marketing hype that every new app or iteration of a product is "the greatest."

Not everything new is good, and not everything old is bad. Focusing only on technologies that enhance our lives is a better approach.

For companies that continue to pursue technologies that cut costs but make the customer experience worse, shame on them. I wonder how many of the technology geniuses who design these systems use them when they need to have a problem solved. It's like a chef who doesn't taste his or her cooking. They wouldn't know that they're serving up crap.

### Lessons from Augusta National Members

"Stewarding good tech is about recognizing our power over technology, using it wisely, and choosing to play the long game."– Ginni Rometty, former CEO, IBM

# CHAPTER THIRTEEN

# Principle #5

# Adopt a Mindset of Continuous Improvement

Denny of Dumbarton, a Scottish shipbuilder, had the idea. So did the eighth shogun, Yoshimune Tokagawa. Although separated by 6,000 miles and a century, the two unlikely thought leaders are bound together by their desire to improve.

Their approaches were radically different. But also, similar. They asked for suggestions on how to make things better. With cash as an incentive.

The shogun put a small box on the entrance to his castle. He had what we would today call a strict set of rules. If you submitted your suggestion via the box, that was good. If an idea was accepted, a reward was given. If you approached him in person, the punishment was decapitation.

The Glasgow shipbuilder wasn't as much of a stickler for rules. He just wanted to keep getting better at building ships with fewer defects. He offered ten pounds for suggestions that made machines work better, reduced waste, or made any process more efficient. There was no risk of losing your head if you approached him directly.

Today, specialists use a series of mundane acronyms to describe continuous improvement: CIP, TQM, and DCAIM.

The Japanese have a catchier term—*kaizen.*

The concept of continuous improvement was reintroduced to the Japanese by Americans during the post-war occupation. It was a philosophy first used broadly by Toyota. Toyota took the radical step of shutting down its production line when it spotted even small problems, allowing them to permanently eliminate issues. Through this iterative process of continual refinement, they excelled at manufacturing cars with minimal defects.

Although Cliff Roberts never expressed his sentiment as *kaizen,* his philosophy of continually improving was a founding principle that the club has embraced through the years. A man of vision, Roberts foresaw a day when Bobby Jones would no longer be the only draw to the tournament. Thus, it "needed to be operated in a better fashion and made more enjoyable than any other."

Roberts was strong-willed and had unyielding views about how the tournament should be run. He established a "Tournament Improvements Committee" early on. Made up of club members and prior Masters winners, each year the committee would make recommendations in a wide range of areas, including how to improve the patron experience, maintain the course better, and make the tournament operate more smoothly. The committee reviewed over fifty suggestions at any given time, with roughly a dozen ready to be implemented when the club had enough money. Roberts laid down this vital pillar, which the tournament still relies on today: "No public event ever stands still, but gets either better or worse. We were determined that our tournament must constantly improve."

A look at the improvements in chronological order shows how seriously the club takes this principle.

Although the property the club acquired to build their dream course on had been a commercial nursery, the trees and bushes were not naturally aligned with where Alister MacKenzie and Jones routed the holes. Looking to improve the course before the Masters was conceived, it was a stroke of genius to choose Louis Alphonse Berckmans and his brother Allie (both sons of P.J.A. Berckmans) to help beautify the course. Louis, a landscape designer, relocated to New York after the nursery closed to work on the landscaping of Rockefeller Center in the early 1930s. Although he was elderly and not a golfer, Louis asked to become a club member and was granted admission. The brothers transplanted over four thousand trees and shrubs to beautify the course. The incorporation of nurserymen into the club's operations—separate from the greenkeepers—was done from the early days. The club established a three-acre nursery, initially under the supervision of Louis and Allie, so they could nurture and grow their own flowering plants.

The tournament's innovations began at the inaugural Masters in 1934, when it was the first to have a radio broadcast carried nationally, with one radio tower provided to CBS.

Underground cabling was also put in place to allow scores to be relayed more quickly by telephone. Traditionally, golf tournaments were held over three days, with the final two rounds played on the third day. The Masters was the first professional tournament held over four days. The idea emanated from Bobby Jones, who knew how straining playing thirty-six holes on the final day could be. In addition to continually refining elements of the tournament, creating creature comforts for patrons was a top priority. In the tournament's fifth year, the club installed pine log benches around the course so spectators could sit and enjoy the golf. The first green jackets were introduced for members during the tournament in 1937. It was not done to make the members look fashionable; it was to make them easy to identify in case patrons needed assistance.

Between the late 1930s and the suspension of the tournament in 1943, several improvements were made. In the early days, players would send out "runners" before the start of play each day to find out where the pins were cut. To improve this cumbersome process, the tournament put pin location placards on every tee so players would know the flag's location without runners. Always thinking about how the press could be treated well, platforms and small towers were put up so better vantage points were available to take photographs. An improvement that has remained unchanged to the current day is the white caddie coveralls, which were instituted in the 1940s at the suggestion of the head professional, Ed Dudley.

When the tournament resumed in 1946, servicemen's badges were introduced, allowing war veterans preferential access to watch the Masters. The Masters was the first tournament to have on-course leader scoreboards, although the early ones were rudimentary, with scores posted in chalk—the operators sat in wooden folding chairs, grasping phones nearby. It wasn't until 1947 that the first scoreboard towers were put in place (another first), although, unlike today's rear-loading scoreboards, scores were loaded from the front, with the operators often blocking out scores. In 1948, the eleventh fairway was roped off—a first. Many tournaments roped off greens and tees prior, but the Masters was the first to rope off fairways. Sam Snead was the first tournament winner to receive a green jacket, an innovation implemented in 1949.

Ben Hogan had the brilliant idea to host a champions dinner in 1952, inviting all previous tournament winners, calling it the "Masters Club Dinner." The first dinner was intimate, with eleven past champions in attendance, accompanied by Jones and Roberts. The Sarazen bridge was installed and dedicated in 1955, and in 1958, the Par 3 course, designed by George Cobb and Cliff Roberts, was opened.

A good way to appreciate how much the Masters has evolved is by looking at historical images of the tournament. Getty Images has many early photographs captured from Augusta National's archives, and the club produced summary films of each tournament (Roberts called them television movies) beginning in 1961. The films were initially created to be seen only by Augusta National members and their guests. Rather than the uniforms worn today, in the '60s and '70s, marshals wore their own clothing, but were easy to identify because of their exotic white pith helmets. The gallery guards operating the ropes were from local colleges and Augusta's military academy—the latter wearing crisp brown uniforms and yellow garrison hats.

The driving range was located to the left of Magnolia Lane, backing up to Washington Road. It was an era before the club hid anything unsightly with shrubs and trees, so rows of cars could be seen along the edge of the driving range. The range itself was scruffy, and caddies stood in the field shagging balls.

The films show imperfections on the course: unsightly bare patches and bunker edges that are rough and untrimmed. Before the club became prickly about the language used, Chris Schenkel, the narrator of the films, called the thick grass rough, because that is exactly what it was. In some areas, it was high and unsightly. Patrons are seen running throughout the film, and when the last group walks up the eighteenth hole, gallery ropes are pulled up behind them, and the crowds rush in British-Open style to pack in and see the action. Hogan Bridge looks different in the early films—less photogenic, with dirt paths on both sides, its rough edges yet to be smoothed out.

Rather than blending in like today, members of the litter crew walked around the course conspicuously, with garbage-picking poles in hand and green satchels slung around their bodies, snatching up litter to put in large, ugly garbage cans. When it rained, the patron viewing areas and dirt paths turned into muddy messes.

To the modern viewer, many things look odd, and they were no doubt abolished by Cliff Roberts when he took notice of them. White station wagons with television cameras affixed to their roofs could be seen on several holes. It was common for caddies to lie on the fringes of greens and on mounds around them, awaiting their players' shots. The

Arrow Shirt Company, one of the television sponsors, had attractive models on the course shooting a commercial just before the tournament started.

The contrast in the old films to today's perfectly choreographed event is jarring and provides a baseline comparison of what was to be improved upon in future years.

The 1960s saw more change than any other decade and greatly improved the patron experience. The single most consequential year of improvements may have been 1960. The Masters became the first tournament to introduce the over-under method of scoring, where scores were shown to spectators as a number relative to par in red or green, rather than as an aggregate score (this was then widely copied by other tournaments because it was easier to understand); it was the first time a champion was interviewed on television, and to top it off, it was also the first year of the Par 3 Contest, won by Sam Snead.

The permanent trophy was introduced when Gary Player won his first green jacket in 1961. In 1962, the first grandstands were erected. Although the British Open had grandstands on the eighteenth hole before Augusta National, the Masters was the first tournament to spread them around, in areas where patrons would have superior course views. No detail went unnoticed, and they were painted green to blend in with the grass.

In 1965, Butler Cabin was used for the first time for a green jacket presentation, with both co-founders present, although by this time, Jones was confined to a wheelchair because of a degenerative spinal disease. In 1966, the Masters was the first-ever golf tournament broadcast in color.

The 1970s brought some of the most important changes to the golf course, focused on improving its presentation, bringing it up to the standard we are familiar with today. In 1970, the club instituted rear-loading scoreboards so patrons would have unobstructed views. Automatic sprinklers were installed in 1971, helping to improve the course's look significantly.

When Cliff Roberts was vacationing in North Carolina's Blue Ridge Mountains in 1975, he visited the Linville Golf Club. He noticed that the bunkers were filled with bright white sand, which turned out not to be sand but feldspar. Roberts described the feldspar as having "a near-perfect uniformity of particles, the stability of placement, and the lack of compaction without being fluffy," and he immediately kicked off a project to fill all of Augusta National's bunkers with it. The feldspar creates such a striking contrast to the lush grass at Augusta National that generations of golfers have returned to their home course to ask their superintendents why their sand doesn't look like Augusta National's.

The golf course has undergone countless improvements over the years, often precipitated by the desire to provide better spectator viewing. The eighth green was initially designed in a punchbowl style, with large mounds surrounding it, ranging from five feet to a monumental twelve feet tall. Patrons would occupy the mounds, as they made ideal viewing locations, but, both for safety reasons and to allow for greater sight lines from grandstands, they were removed. Ron Whitten and Chris O'Riley analyzed the changes made to the golf course for *Golf Digest*. They identified one hundred changes since it was built, with modifications on at least seven holes precipitated by the desire to provide better spectating for patrons.

Cliff Roberts died in 1977, and it was a significant loss because the need for continual improvement was part of his DNA. It would be decades before the pace of innovations would return to the rate at which he implemented them. After Roberts's death, some chairmen were change-oriented, others less so. Unfortunately, his successor, Bill Lane, fell ill shortly after becoming chairman, so there were few innovations during his tenure.

Hord Hardin became chairman in 1980, and the pace of innovations remained slow. A conservative lawyer from St. Louis, he was serious and awkward in public. Only a handful of changes were made over the twelve years he was at the helm, the biggest of which was allowing USA Network to broadcast two hours of coverage on Thursday and Friday, beginning in 1982—the first major championship to air on cable television. During a Champions Dinner, Arnold Palmer complained to Hardin that mowing the fairways in two directions prevented the ball from rolling forward if a drive were hit against the grain. From that point forward, they were mowed in one direction, although in the opposite manner Palmer requested (the player hits against the grain now). While not a benefit for the players, it had the unintended effect of creating a pleasing aesthetic—the fairway uniformity we recognize today with no gradations.

Jack Stephens took over as chairman in 1991. A native of Little Rock, Arkansas, and a graduate of the Naval Academy, Stephens was an investment banker. His approach to improvements was conservative.

After the slow pace of innovation under the tenures of Lane, Hardin, and Stephens, the pace of innovation accelerated again in 1998 under Hootie Johnson. Most of the improvements made during his tenure were related to changing the golf course, specifically, lengthening it in reaction to Tiger Woods's historic 1997 victory when he finished eighteen strokes under par. Worry set in among the club's leaders, who were concerned about the course becoming obsolete in an era of stronger players and better equipment.

Billy Payne became chairman in 2006 and instituted substantial improvements to the tournament—the most since Cliff Roberts. He instituted patron surveys on the course and online to better understand what changes would improve the tournament, demonstrating that he was willing to be a change agent. Payne was an advocate of growing the game, and in conjunction with the USGA and the R&A, he helped launch both the Asia-Pacific Amateur Championship and the Drive, Chip & Putt. He also improved the patron and player experiences by building the new driving range; and he made the significant investment of building "the Oz within Oz," Berckmans Place. He was at the helm when both the new golf shop and media center were built. Other improvements in the 2010s were centered around technology, with launches of several social media channels.

Chairman Ridley, who assumed control in 2017, also seems to be an innovator and change agent. Under his tenure, he launched the Women's Amateur, implemented the practice of capturing every shot on every hole for the app and website, added the Masters podcast, allowed the use of drones, and opened the Map & Flag hospitality venue. Since he is progressive in his vision, we are likely to see more innovations during his tenure.

One could argue that the Masters has an unfair advantage over other golf tournaments because it is held on the same course every year. This is true when comparing the Masters to the other majors, which rotate from venue to venue. When looked at broadly, the Masters is in the same position as many different tournaments, where golf is held on the same course every year. What sets the Masters apart is their ongoing commitment to improvement every year.

Charles Price wrote, "When the tournament is over, groups of [members] sit down in the clubhouse and perhaps have a drink together to discuss how the event worked out. There is seldom a sense of self-satisfaction among them. Then they go home . . . trying to dream up one more tiny improvement for the next year's event, one more little thing, however imperceptible, that might give the Masters Tournament that final dab of polish that will say, There! Now you're perfect. None of them cares that virtually everyone who follows tournaments in person or on television thinks the Masters already is about as perfect a golf tournament can get."

A key takeaway is the consistency the club applies to this principle. Embracing continuous improvement has become a hallmark of the Masters. The club has worked hard at it for almost one hundred years, and we can anticipate that they will continue to do so into the future.

# CHAPTER FOURTEEN

# How to Adopt a Mindset of Continuous Improvement

Toyota was one of the first large companies to focus on continuous improvement as a key part of their business strategy. Their way of doing business, now known as the Toyota Production System (TPS), has been emulated worldwide. The company still operates under the philosophy that "all employees implement daily incremental *kaizen*." The most important part of what Toyota has done is to make continuous improvement a part of its culture. Rather than viewing employees who point out defects as complainers, they embrace them.

The Korean electronics manufacturer Samsung also has continuous improvement deeply ingrained in its culture. They don't express it as *kaizen*, as Toyota does, but instead they have adapted the Six Sigma method of statistical analysis, continually adjusting how they operate, seeking an error-free rate in their processes and end products of 99.9997 percent.

The medical profession is another that strives to improve continually across all areas at all times, although one of the most impressive organizations that does this consistently is the U.S. Military.

## U.S. Military

Without embracing continual change and trying to outsmart potential adversaries, our Armed Forces would forever be thinking about how to fight the last war. Instead, they are always looking ahead. "We aim to seed, spark, and stoke the flames of innovation," Deputy Defense Secretary Kathleen Hicks said. She continued, "We use American ingenuity: our ability to think freely, innovate, change the game, and in the military sphere, to imagine, create, and master the future character of warfare." The Department of Defense collaborates with some of the leading universities in the country, including Carnegie Mellon, MIT, and the University of California, to help advance its research and innovation capabilities so that it can continually improve and be on the cutting edge. In 2006, the Department of Defense instituted a continuous process improvement program spanning its entire organization.

Two small examples of how it's used: The Marine Corps uses a set of innovation and process improvement tools to enhance combat readiness so it can provide the best support to its warfighters; the Air Force uses a continuous process to improve maintenance of the B-2 Stealth Bomber, resulting in a more reliable aircraft. Using technology wisely and continually improving often go hand-in-hand, which is why the military has some of the most sophisticated technology ever created. The continuous improvement doctrine of the military has led to many life-changing innovations that were then applied outside its domain, including the creation of the Internet (via the Defense Advanced Research Projects Agency), the GPS, drones, weather radar, bug spray, duct tape, and microwave ovens.

Since Bobby Jones and Clifford Roberts both served in the Army, it's no surprise that the Masters operates with military precision.

## Apple

The Japanese broadcaster NHK produced a documentary examining Steve Jobs's life, detailing his lifelong fascination with the country and how it changed him, including "his religion, his diet, his fashion, and his design philosophy." Jobs visited Japan over a dozen times and studied how Sony operated in detail. John Sculley, CEO of Apple for a decade, witnessed his obsessiveness: "Jobs was a freak about Sony." He modeled Apple after Sony, copying their attention to detail and ingraining a philosophy of continually improving into the culture. He was impressed with how spotlessly clean Sony's factories were, and he designed Apple's Macintosh factories to mirror theirs. A prime example of the company's focus on continuous improvement is the approach taken with the iPhone camera. First introduced in 2007, every year or two the features are improved, often dramatically, to the point that serious photographers now use the cameras.

A Harvard Business School case study focusing on Apple describes how their organizational structure contributes not only to their ability to improve continually, but also highlights their adherence to some other principles, especially what they refer to as a "fanatical attention to detail." Rather than using an organizational structure based on business units like most companies, the company is organized along functional lines instead, creating an organization of experts instead of generalists. "One principle that permeates Apple is 'Leaders should know the details of their organization three levels down,'" the study says. In addition to its organizational structure, Apple uses a proprietary architecture and is paranoid about control. This gives them a competitive advantage over companies that follow a more "open" model. It is a Cliff Roberts level of control.

Apple's leaders are as obsessive as Jobs. Scott Forstall, a senior executive working at the company when they were developing the iPhone, kept a "jeweler's loupe in his office to check every pixel on every icon," looking for imperfections.

When Tim Cook became CEO, there were endless comparisons to Steve Jobs. Would he be as strategic? Would he be the product genius or the showman that Jobs was? The answer was no, but that's not what Apple needed. Cook made his mark at Apple as the supply-chain guy. Boring stuff, but again, "God is in the details." That's what Cook still excels at—keeping Apple a great, detail-focused company. Package designers at Apple spend months toiling over the smallest details of the packaging, whereas many companies view the packaging as an afterthought. When the iPod launched, they tried hundreds of different boxes so that the designers could experience what customers would. They tried "an endless series of arrows, colors, and tapes for a tiny tab designed to show the customer where to pull." It's a great example of using continuous improvement to learn and progress.

Tim Cook summarizes a core part of Apple's strategy: "We're perfectly fine with not being first," he says. "As it turns out, it takes a while to get it really great. It takes a lot of iteration. It takes worrying about every detail."

Why don't more organizations or people adopt a mindset of continuous improvement? Because it's hard to do on a sustained basis, particularly for companies that don't manufacture products. *Kaizen* is also a difficult process for individuals to adapt to. New Year's resolutions are a prime example. Anthony Raymond, author of a book about *kaizen*, recommends trying to implement change by setting small goals and then building on them incrementally. For example, after setting a goal to exercise more, he recommends intentionally parking further away in a parking lot to force a longer walk. Doing so sends the correct signals to the brain and makes it easier to do more the next day.

| Lessons from Augusta National Members |
|---|
| "I am not in competition with anyone but myself. My goal is to improve myself continuously." – Bill Gates |

# CHAPTER FIFTEEN

# Principle #6

# Treat People with Respect

Treating people with respect shouldn't be that hard. It's a basic principle every parent teaches their children. It's the Golden Rule. The Masters stands out because they have institutionalized treating people with respect. They respect television viewers by not bombarding them with advertising. At the tournament, they show respect even before patrons enter the gates with free parking. It extends to their reasonable food and drink prices. And to the consideration given by Augusta National members enthusiastically welcoming patrons into the tournament. And the security guards doing the same. The courtesies extend from the minute you park your car until you leave the property.

During the 1968 Masters the Argentine golfer Roberto De Vicenzo finished with the same score as Bob Goalby, but signed for the wrong score on his scorecard. He signed for a sixty-six instead of the sixty-five he shot, but under the Rules of Golf, "a score higher than actually played must stand as returned." There was a lot of discussion when the error was brought to light, and ultimately, the head of the rules committee brought the issue to Bobby Jones to see if there was anything they could do to overlook the issue and have a playoff. As a private invitational tournament, why couldn't they have a local rule to ignore the infraction? Jones's answer was short and to the point: "Boys, you know the Rules of Golf. Goalby wins the tournament." This is entirely consistent with Jones's life. It was a painful decision, and Jones called it "Tragic beyond expression. I like to think, though, that it served one useful purpose in emphasizing the respect which golfers must have for the rule book."

Free parking at the Masters was enshrined from the beginning, a point Roberts took pride in. "This inducement was an immeasurable stimulant to the sale of tickets," he said of the parking. Likewise, complimentary pairing sheets were given out, rather than charging for programs, an early example of the underlying principle of putting patrons first. Roberts also established the philosophy of setting up the course in a fan-friendly fashion. The U.S. Open approaches its tournament from the opposite perspective and strives to test all aspects of a player's game by creating carnage, severely penalizing missed shots. "Those who patronize the Masters get more pleasure and excitement watching the great players make birdies than bogies," Roberts wrote in *The Story of Augusta National.* "We could set up the course so that no one could break eighty, but we are certain such a policy would be unpopular with the patrons."

While Augusta National has woven respect into all aspects of how it operates, large companies seem to have done the opposite. Although it is the Golden Rule, does it feel like airports treat hapless travelers with respect when they have to shell out $6 for a bottle of water that costs twelve cents? Or when we get a notice that a company is "updating their terms of service," when what they are doing is raising prices, but they don't say so because they don't respect our intelligence. Or when we sit in a doctor's office waiting for thirty minutes because they don't respect our time? My definition of respect in the context of this chapter is broad. It includes institutionalized disrespect, that is, companies or institutions that think they are doing a great job treating customers well, when their business models are substandard and disrespectful.

"We're experiencing unusually high call volumes, but we appreciate your business; please continue to hold." Translation: "We've decided to prioritize making money over providing good service, so you'll be on hold listening to irritating music for the next thirty minutes." It's a choice companies make—keep profit margins high or provide better service. Automated call trees are another tactic employed and are simply a way to discourage us from speaking with a person. "Press one, press two, press twelve, press fifteen, and then, because our technology has bugs in it, you'll be disconnected." It is disrespectful, and a choice companies make repeatedly. It's funny how some companies have had unusually high call volumes for years.

Moving call centers to the Philippines and India is another way large companies show disdain for us. I want to be crystal clear that I have nothing against Indians and

Filipinos, or any other ethnic group. They are hardworking people trying to make a living for themselves and their families, just like we all are. My issue is with the companies that have set up their outsourced support in a way that institutionalizes disregard for customers.

There are problems with commonsense solutions they choose to ignore: fix the phone connections so there is no static and we can hear each other halfway around the world without the need to spell your name over and over; staff the phones with individuals who have excellent communication skills in English, rather than those that struggle with the language; burn the scripts they are reading from and give them the authority to talk to us like we are human beings, instead of acting like robots. Do those three things, and I'm all in on outsourcing wherever a company wants. But that's not the way the world works today.

The decision is facilitated by a bean counter with a spreadsheet, who shows a short-sighted executive how much money they will save. There is no way to quantify how much it will irritate and disrespect customers in the spreadsheet, so it seems like an easy decision to outsource.

The problem is not limited to companies that have outsourced their operations. Those still based in the U.S. can be equally pitiful. You know it's not going to be a good experience when the first words you hear when calling your utility company are, "Welcome to our automated assistant. I'm here to help you today." Uh-oh, you're not; you're here to keep me from speaking to someone. What strikes me about the current generation of automated assistants is that they are hard of hearing. "I'm sorry, I didn't hear you." Or, "I'm sorry, I don't understand." Okay. I hit the pound key and the number zero in rapid succession, and sometimes this gets me past these dreadful systems. "Before I can transfer you to an agent, I'll need more information," seems to be the latest version of them, and they are simply additional obstacles that have been put between the by-now-weary customer and an agent. After spending five minutes sparring with the automated assistant, then finally hitting the right combination of buttons, the ultimate in disrespect is announced: "We have an average wait time of between forty and sixty minutes." This is not a hypothetical example, but one I had recently when calling my electricity provider, FirstEnergy Corporation, whose revenues in 2023 were $12.8 billion. Is it too much to ask them to adequately staff their phone lines and treat customers with more respect? With $12.8 billion in revenue, there should be enough money to hire additional talent. I've given up calling UPS because their call center agents in whatever far-flung location they are in have the worst combination of poor language skills and an unwavering commitment to sticking to their mind-numbing scripts.

In a survey conducted in 2002, 65 percent of respondents said they don't even bother calling customer service eight-hundred numbers anymore because it is so painful. The average time on hold is an energy-sapping forty-two minutes. And this is the kicker: three calls are typically required to resolve an issue. More than a quarter of respondents would prefer to go to the dentist or the DMV, rather than experiencing the slow, painful process of dealing with the roadblocks the companies have set up. How about having to repeat your name and account number, and other verifying details when you are transferred to another representative after finally getting through? By any measure, it makes customers feel devalued and not appreciated.

The flip side, which seems to be lost on most large companies, is that 80 percent of respondents said their opinion of a brand or company would increase if they had a positive experience calling customer service. A *Wall Street Journal* article cited an estimate that Americans collectively spent 900 million hours on hold in 2024.

It doesn't take much of a cynical view to conclude that the whole experience is designed to put us off so we don't bother the companies. What if we applied the "do unto others" rule and put the CEOs of these companies on hold for forty to sixty minutes of their day? Would they fix the phone support then?

Leaders of big companies have become detached and never experience their own support systems or products, so it seems unlikely to change. They need to get out more. Only then would they realize that, like many things in life, more things sound good in theory than work in the real world. Augusta National members are on the property supervising every aspect of the Masters in person. It's a good model for leaders to follow. Not every day, because that becomes micromanagement. But at least periodically, as a reality check, to ensure they aren't only being fed positive information by underlings eager to please.

Quite a bit of the corporate disrespect we now suffer from can be traced back to a movement led by the "Chicago School" of economics, a group of academics at the University of Chicago. Among other gifts the 1970s gave us were lava lamps, shag carpets, and Richard Nixon. We can add to the list a new philosophy adopted by large corporations, and the genesis of how disrespect has become institutionalized. In 1970, Nobel Prize-winning economist and University of Chicago professor Milton Friedman wrote an article arguing that the only "social responsibility of business is to increase its profits." Prior to the 1970s it was generally believed that corporations and businesses served three constituents: their owners, their customers, and the communities they operated in.

"The Friedman Doctrine," as it came to be known, shifted the balance toward profitability, putting corporate short-termism out front. This sparked a fire in the business world, which has lately become an all-encompassing blaze, devaluing consumers at the expense of the quest for continual profit growth. Andrew Ross Sorkin wrote an important article for the *New York Times* several years ago, interviewing a dozen leading academics and business leaders, questioning the wisdom of the Friedman Doctrine. Martin Lipton, a senior partner at Wachtell, Lipton, Rosen & Katz, has been dubbed one of the "100 Most Influential Lawyers in America." Lipton told Sorkin, "This version of capitalism was ascendant in the 1980s and continued until the 2008 financial crisis, when the perils of short-termism were vividly illustrated and the long-term economic and societal harms of shareholder primacy were becoming increasingly urgent." Alex Gorsky, chief executive of Johnson & Johnson, also weighed in, "In 1943, as Johnson & Johnson prepared for its initial public offering, Robert Wood Johnson made clear our responsibilities as a corporation: first to the patients, doctors and nurses, mothers and fathers and others who use our products and services, then to our customers and business partners, our employees and our communities. And finally, to our shareholders." Notice where shareholders landed in his description of the company's priorities.

I recently called Comcast to downgrade my service since they raise prices every year. The experience was awful.

When I call Comcast and press the button that says I want to buy or upgrade my service, I am connected to an employee reasonably fast. When I call and press the button to downgrade or cancel services, not so much. Those upgrade and purchase calls are a priority because they can hear the cash registers ringing. After a long delay on hold while trying to downgrade, I was finally connected to an employee and was subjected to five minutes of attempts to upsell me to other products. It wasn't pleasant, but the company forces you to cancel services by calling them. There is no option on their phone tree to downgrade or cancel, and no way to do it online. It is intentionally designed to treat us like second-class citizens, devaluing our time, in the hope that we will give up and go do something more productive.

I've read that Starbucks is one of the companies in the U.S. with the highest customer satisfaction. Their technology drives part of that. Their app is good—we can customize an order, are notified when it is ready, and can walk in (or drive through) and pick it up. It works well. That falls under the convenience category and shows that they respect our time, but other aspects of their business are sorely lacking. The last time I bought food from Starbucks, it was old and stale. I bought a scone that showed a date on the package indicating that it was three months old. An iced lemon loaf was two months old and tasteless. Both were made in some factory on the other side of the continent, frozen, and then defrosted. Their coffee is good, but their food products are terrible.

If Starbucks had a mindset of treating its customers with respect, its food would taste good, like that of its competitor, Dunkin'. Or like the egg salad, pimento cheese, and barbeque sandwiches at the Masters, which are fresh.

Cliff Roberts wrote about the early days of the Masters, "We believe that one of the reasons the Masters is popular with patrons of the game is because they can obtain good food and drink at reasonable prices." The reasonable pricing is refreshing because it has become rare. The sandwich prices at the Masters range from $1.50 to $3.00, and a beer is $5.00, compared to a barbeque sandwich and a beer at the U.S. Open, which cost $11.00 each.

The pricing at the Masters feels good because our sense of trust has eroded at so many places. The default assumption is that we won't be treated fairly. When we are, it's a legitimate shock. Allow me to air some grievances. UPS instituted a fuel surcharge when gas prices spiked. Fair enough. When gas prices dropped, it became as sticky as flypaper. What's with "handling fees" increasingly seen when buying online? Doesn't the shipping charge cover the cost of getting the item to us? It's rude. Look closely at your cable bill, "Regulatory Cost Recovery Fee." It's not a tax, but a backhanded way for Comcast to charge more. International airline tickets have a "U.S. Customs User Fee" and a "U.S. Immigration User Fee." I was under the mistaken belief that my federal taxes paid for all these agencies. A $40 fee to check a bag. It's price gouging.

When companies focus on profitability first and foremost, instead of viewing customers as real people with busy lives who don't have an unlimited ability to pay up, it erodes a sense of balance, and they slowly begin treating us with less respect. As difficult as it is to remember, there was a time not that long ago when it was possible to call a company (even a large one) and a knowledgeable person would pick up the phone reasonably quickly and speak to you. And when companies would say in plain English that they were raising prices. It is the toxic combination of the Friedman Doctrine, married with technologies that are used not to help, but to dissuade, that has created our modern era of depersonalized, crappy service. Consumers have become so sick of this that savvy businesses have figured out it is now a significant advantage to talk to their customers without all these impediments.

The green jacket ceremony is an integral part of the Masters. How the club approaches it shows how ingrained their respect is for their employees. A little-noticed, but important part of the ceremony, is that each year the club selects an employee to walk out and present the green jacket. The Green Jacket Award of Excellence, it is called, and in 2022 the award recipient was Ike Stokes, a maintenance employee who began working for Augusta National in 1972, with the longest service record of any employee in the club's history. Stokes is responsible for irrigation and green maintenance. Stokes has the best lunch routine in the world. Rather than sitting at a desk or in a drab cafeteria, he sits near the twelfth green to enjoy his lunch. He was given the honor, in part because "he helps pass on our respect for tradition by sharing our history and the experience he has gained over five decades." The 2023 recipient was chef Eddie Davis, who said, "It just means the world to me." In 2024, the club selected Ronnie L. Stuckey, their chief security guard, to do the honors. A veteran of Operation Desert Storm, Stuckey said, "It's a proud moment for the club, for my team, and for me and my family. I'll never forget it, and I'm sure they won't either."

Respect. It pays off in so many ways.

It isn't only companies or organizations that have devalued respect; it is also individuals. The "new" disrespect in our computer age is not New York-style in-your-face, but a subtler form. When I was in the corporate world, it drove me crazy when someone was trying to reach me, and it appeared urgent. They would call my landline, and if I didn't pick up, they would call my cell phone. If I didn't answer, I would get a text message, and sometimes even an email on top of that. *Oh my,* I thought, *I hope no one has died; this seems really urgent.* And then when I finally connected with the knucklehead, it wasn't urgent at all. It's that the person either didn't have enough respect for themselves or for me to put the urgency of their issue in context.

The medical profession provides another example. Unfortunately, I have had to visit dozens of doctors over the last few years as I was recovering from leukemia and the lingering side effects of a bone marrow transplant. Without exaggeration, I have seen forty specialists across various medical disciplines. The more experienced doctors look you in the eye, and you have a conversation. The less experienced, newly trained doctors look at their computer screens and type notes while you interact with them. I'm sure hospitals and insurance companies put a ton of administrative burdens on them, and it saves time later, but it is disrespectful. The sad part is, they are not doing it intentionally; they just don't seem to know better.

The most commonsense and obvious conclusion regarding the principle of treating people with respect is that it is a choice that both companies and people make. Augusta National runs a master class in respect. They've made it a core principle, integrating it into everything they do. Chairman Ridley articulates it well: "There's something about Augusta National when someone walks through the gates, they know that it's a place of respect." Contrast that with, "There's something about dealing with Comcast, FirstEnergy, Starbucks, and UPS that makes you feel like you're Rodney Dangerfield." That's a fake quote I made up, but it drives home the point. People who pay money to attend the Masters are called patrons, a special term whose meaning is lost on many large companies who have lost the narrative.

They no longer understand that when customers are treated with respect, they will respect a brand and a company more, showing loyalty instead of being disgusted by them.

# CHAPTER SIXTEEN

# How to Treat People with Respect

It's not a good feeling at the DMV when we're told that we didn't fill out the correct form and must fill out a new form, then head to the back of the line. The opposite feeling is invoked when we're treated the right way, highlighted by a couple of stalwart organizations below.

**Publix**

Publix Super Markets, based in Florida, with a thousand stores in the Southeast, is a good example of a company that has a culture that balances their profitability with serving customers respectfully. Their stores are well-laid-out and clean, and their prices are reasonable. Similar to attending the Masters, almost all their associates are cheery and treat customers with good manners. Part of the secret of Publix's success is that they are employee-owned (employees own 80 percent of the company, and the founding family the other 20), and thus they don't have to bow to the same pressures as the publicly owned companies I used as examples of poor service. "We try to manage with servant leadership, and you have to lead with passion," says Publix Super Markets executive chairman Todd Jones. Servant leadership is not a phrase heard often.

Publix is one of the largest privately held companies in the U.S., employing over 250,000 people, and they operate with a culture of respect. The University of Richmond Robins School of Business highlighted Publix in a case study: "[George] Jenkins, the company's founder, called on each Publix employee to 'make each customer's day a little bit better because they met you.'" That mantra continues to shape the behavior of Publix employees even today. Employees embrace Publix's "ten-foot" and "ten-second" rules: speaking to and smiling at every customer within ten feet, and greeting customers within the first ten seconds of their arrival in a department. And instead of giving customers aisle numbers to find an item, Publix employees are trained to get the item for the customer. Publix has implemented a "two-customers-per-line" goal to ensure shoppers move quickly through checkout. Publix regularly ranks as one of *Fortune's* Best 100 Companies to Work For and is ranked first in *Newsweek's* Best Customer Service in the Supermarket category. Ticking even more boxes, the company operates with a Continuous Quality Improvement (CQI) program, and their employee turnover rate is a mind-bogglingly low 5 percent.

## Disney

Like Publix, Disney has also created a respectful culture for both its associates and its guests. Lee Cockerell, a former executive vice president at Disney World, was responsible for running the park, and discusses the concept at length in his excellent book, *Creating Magic*: "People will not remember what you said, they will remember how you made them feel. Create an inspiring vocabulary that makes people feel respected." Lee was responsible for 40,000 cast members, and he made sure that the ticket takers, parking lot attendants, the people who cleaned the bathrooms, and those who emptied the garbage cans, were all treated with the same respect as the cast members who interacted with guests. The culture Cockerell describes made Disney the most reputable company in the world, as ranked by *Fortune* in 2024. Lee was a very senior executive, yet whenever he met with someone in his office, he made it a point to stand up, come around to the other side of the desk, and sit next to them.

I always did the same; it is a small gesture, but it shows no one is better than anyone else. Working on Wall Street for twenty years, I could tell when someone had an elevated sense of self-importance and would likely be a jerk when they sat behind their desk as a show of power. My worst disrespectful behavior experience was a meeting with a member of the Executive Committee at Morgan Stanley— someone who reported to the chairman. A small group of us showed up for a meeting with him. He was so arrogant that he made us sit in a little conference room adjacent to his office, while he remained in his office, and we held the meeting via a conference call.

Beyond respecting its cast members and guests, Disney, like Ritz-Carlton, ticks many boxes on the other principles. Their attention to detail in the parks and their products is well-known, and it was an outgrowth of the tone set by the founder, Walt Disney. When Disneyland first opened in 1955, the maker of the first stagecoach to appear in the park was having difficulty getting the straps to look precisely as Walt wanted them to look. He asked, "Why don't we just leave the leather straps off, Walt? The people are never going to appreciate all this close-up detail." Disney responded, "They will respond to it. They will appreciate it. And they will keep coming back to the park again, and again, and again." Disney has an eye-popping 70 percent guest return rate.

Disney has made many efforts to give back (principle eight) and support veterans over the last century. Although Walt Disney was too young to enlist when World War I broke out, he joined the Red Cross Ambulance Corps. As the war was winding down, he served as an ambulance driver in France, the same role Cliff Roberts had. Disney offers members of the military discounts on park tickets, and they have hired 15,000 veterans as part of a Heroes Work Here program launched in 2012.

Since I like clean bathrooms, it won't surprise you that manhole covers are another thing for me. In the same vein that the Masters carves their logo into doors and tabletops, even when it's unnecessary, the manhole covers at Walt Disney World have images of Mickey Mouse in the middle. Joshua Gans, a professor at the University of Toronto, notes the similarities between Apple and Disney regarding their attention to detail. At Apple, "there is the desire to make the insides of computers beautiful even though no one will see them. With the mouse on the manhole cover, we see the same thing at Disney: details that don't need to be there." It's what separates companies that are middle-of-the-pack from those that are revered.

Disney's technology strategy is commendable, particularly in the movie business, with continual innovations and the use of cutting-edge technologies. The parallels to merchandising are also notable, with Disney and the Masters being two of the best in the business. Their honoring of the past (principle nine) is self-evident, by keeping alive characters such as Mickey Mouse, Donald Duck, and Snow White, that less-enlightened companies would have downplayed long ago.

## The Atlanta Falcons

The Atlanta Falcons are an excellent sports comparable to the Masters. When the team built its new stadium in 2017, they modeled it after the Masters and wanted it to be "the best experience in sports." They lowered food and beverage prices so a hot dog costs only $2.00, and a beer, only $5.00. Joe Pompliano explains the strategy in his *Huddle Up* newsletter: "Many owners initially thought Arthur Blank was crazy for introducing this 'fan first' pricing menu. TV rights will always be the most critical line item on a team's balance sheet, but concessions still bring in about $2 million per game for an NFL team. This ended up having the opposite effect, though. By building out more kiosks to reduce wait times and keeping concession prices consistent across every event, including the Super Bowl, Arthur Blank revolutionized the stadium experience." The result—fan satisfaction increased, as did merchandise sales. And the lower prices were more than offset by higher volumes, with concession spending increasing. The approach the Falcons took in their new stadium is the best one-to-one comparison to how the Masters operates. It shows how adopting some of Augusta National's principles leads to better outcomes.

Treating customers better requires companies to get two elements right: the first is to institute a true culture of service.

The Masters is at the apex of this, with everyone who interacts with a patron trained to focus on making them happy. And for the second element, companies must experience the horror of horrors. Wait for it. They have to spend more money and reduce their profit margins. It means hiring more people in call centers or hiring more cashiers to make checkout quicker. While spending more money may be counterintuitive, businesses make more in the long run because customers embrace the brand more.

Many companies give lip service to the concept of putting customers first, and their outward-facing publicity is full of platitudes and empty promises. But when push comes to shove, they make their decisions based on a spreadsheet.

### Lessons from Augusta National Members

"May we all pledge to respect each other." – Condoleezza Rice, former U.S. Secretary of State

# CHAPTER SEVENTEEN

# Principle #7

# Cultivate Civility

Who is dumber than a doorknob, has zero emotional intelligence, and relishes in behaving in an uncouth manner? In the South, they have a shorthand description for this despicable character: a dumbass. In Britain, they call him a tosser. The long-form answer is the drunken fool who shows up at a golf tournament and screams at the top of his lungs, "get in the hole," and the inexplicable, "mashed potatoes" after a golf shot is hit.

A spectator suggestion booklet, prepared by Bobby Jones, and given out to patrons reads, "In golf, customs of etiquette and decorum are just as important as the rules governing play. It is appropriate for spectators to applaud successful strokes in proportion to difficulty, but excessive demonstrations by a player or his partisans are not proper because of the possible effect upon other competitors. Most distressing to those who love the game is the applauding or cheering of misplays or misfortunes of a player. Such occurrences have been rare at the Masters but we must eliminate them entirely if our patrons are to continue to merit their reputation as the most knowledgeable and considerate in the world."

One of the essential principles that makes the Masters special is that all the patrons behave in a civilized manner, creating a calm and tranquil environment. I've heard the Masters described as the world's biggest day spa, which paints just the right portrait. It took decades for the tournament to perfect its soothing environment, and they achieved it through a process of elimination, specifically by eliminating unwanted noises. Keeping noise to a minimum allows patrons to enjoy the beauty of the property more by reducing stress.

Eliminating a blimp takes away humming and whirring sounds from above. There are no generators powering scoreboards or concession stands, further reducing background noise, and aside from an occasional golf cart riding through, there are no noises from motor vehicles.

The fence around the property and the buffer zone created by the trees and shrubs ringing the course shield patrons from the din of the outside world. One of the most significant contributors to the calm environment is the lack of cell phones, eliminating the booming voices people inexplicably use when talking on them. There has been speculation for years that the bird noises heard in person and by television viewers are piped in and artificially created. They're not. And it's a sad commentary that when we slow down and remove the interferences of modern life from the picture, and can hear birdsong, we suspect something is wrong. Nothing is wrong; this is the world as it should be.

The guidelines of etiquette and decorum provided by Bobby Jones and reinforced every year play a part in setting the tone in the appropriate manner, but so do the rules. The environment being impeccably maintained is equally important. Another committee Cliff Roberts established was a "Grounds and Litter Control Committee." A serious venture, the committee was initially run by a retired brigadier general, a major general, and a lieutenant colonel, directing a staff of about fifty. Roberts took great pride in noting, "The clean-up operation has been a feature of the Masters since its inception, and our patrons co-operate to a remarkable extent. It is not uncommon to see a spectator go out of his way to pick up a paper cup or other form of litter and then place it where it belongs in a trash bag."

Roberts and the committee were ahead of their time in their approach. In 1982, the "Broken Windows Theory" was advanced by two social scientists who posited that focusing on enforcement of minor crimes, such as littering and graffiti, would have an outsized impact on improving overall crime rates. This, in turn, would have a positive impact on the social order within neighborhoods. Several large cities, including New York, implemented the theory, and it reduced overall crime. While the theory has its critics, and it can be overdone, the same underlying principle is what Roberts notes in his comment about patrons recognizing how spotless the environment is at the Masters, and how it creates a positive feedback loop and sense of pride, motivating patrons to help keep it pristine.

Focusing on the small things has a multiplier effect and creates an environment where the big things take care of themselves. The fact that patrons can't run, can't lie down, can't wear a hat backwards, and can't yell may seem overbearing, but they provide the basis for a decorous event. You would no sooner run or raise your voice in a library or a church than you would at the Masters.

David Coggins, the author of *Men and Manners,* describes part of the Masters secret sauce, "It requires an unspoken collective agreement by everybody in attendance. The resulting atmosphere is both exhilarating but incredibly civilized." He also expresses how the conventions at the tournament, "brings out everybody's better nature, which is worth aspiring to no matter where we are. When people share a sense of occasion, they put forward an ideal version of themselves."

In the same way that we have become numb to wave after wave of advertising, we have also become numb to the noisy world we live in, which is why the serenity of the Masters is something we soak up. When I worked in New York City, I walked a dozen blocks from Penn Station to my office near Grand Central. The cacophony of noises was grating: taxis honking horns incessantly, police and fire engine sirens, the beeping of trucks backing up, garbage trucks emptying dumpsters, the screeching of subway trains heard through the street grates, jackhammers, pile drivers drilling into the bedrock as new towers were built, traffic helicopters overhead, and cement mixers pouring concrete. This is an extreme example, but the sounds of lawn mowers and leaf blowers have become equally irksome in the suburbs.

The same increased level of noise exists in indoor environments. It's rare to find a coffee shop, restaurant, hotel lobby, retail store, airport, or fast-food outlet where rock music isn't playing, often loudly. I know I'm picking on Starbucks, but when I stopped every morning on the way to work to order coffee (before app ordering was prevalent), more often than not, I would have to repeat my order because the server couldn't hear me over the music. Starbucks must let each store pick its music, and since there were a half-dozen stores within a five-minute walk, I tried out several until I found one where they could hear me.

The twenty-first century has been a golden age of technological advancement. Think of what we now take for granted from just our cell phones. We can browse the web, buy products, play games, and gamble with them. They provide us with weather forecasts, navigation, a camera, a clock, a stopwatch, a flashlight, and a recording device. But they are also a major annoyance. Lack of phone etiquette is at the root of much ill-mannered behavior because using a cell phone has somehow become an excuse to speak at a volume that is out of proportion with polite norms, causing a loss of personal space. And the ill-mannered practice of staring at your phone instead of paying attention while someone is talking to you has spun out of control.

The lack of intimacy created by technology has decreased our overall sense of propriety. Twitter is a good example. It thrives on conflict and hostility with clickbait headlines and provocative content. People write things on social media that they would rarely say to a person's face. In addition to cell phones and Twitter contributing to incivility, MSNBC and Fox News both launched in 1996, contributing significantly to the "us versus them" world we now find ourselves in. We no longer disagree with someone; now they are our enemy.

It's no wonder that when we get into the cocoon of the Masters, we're in a better mood and our standards revert to politeness and a lower volume. Not being bombarded with noise is a pleasure, and part of the Masters lore. The Southern accents help, and it's hard to resist greetings of "How y'all doin?" and replies of "Yes ma'am," and "Yes sir" throughout the day. It is contagious and leads to more good behavior.

The opposite of the Masters is LIV golf, whose tagline is "Golf, but louder." LIV tournaments are outfitted with 160 speakers playing music throughout the day, including while players hit their shots. When LIV visited Tulsa, Oklahoma, a local television reporter described the environment: "The second fans walk through the gate they'll hear the sounds and music of LIV, and it won't stop." The director of event production for LIV, A. J. Dolan, talks about the league's operating philosophy: "Our approach is to treat it like an NBA game, or an NHL game or NFL game, where the entire course is integrated like an arena, where every speaker is the same, you hear music on the first hole and you hear music on the eighteenth hole." (Memo to A.J.: Professional sports turn off the music when the games are in progress.) Is this the future of tournament golf? It looks unlikely based on the size of the audiences attending the tournaments and their television audiences.

I picked a representative comment from Reddit from a fan who attended a LIV event, and they weren't impressed: "The very loud and annoying background noise, especially the music, is unbearable." And this comment from an attendee posted on the GolfWRX discussion group: "The constant drone of music became a bit much." John Hawkins of *Sports Illustrated* tuned in to a television broadcast and concluded the best way to watch was on mute: "It's kind of like a five-hour episode of *Hee Haw*, if you dare to imagine such a thing. One inane joke after another, purporting the notion that golf announcers make excellent comedians, with live music blaring in the background for lengthy stretches of the telecast."

My impressions of LIV are not based on my personal experience, because I put them in the triple-never category.

Never been to a tournament. Never watched on television. Never will.

When controversial issues arise in golf, I find one of the best ways to evaluate them is by looking back at traditions and history as a guide. I ask a simple question: What would Bobby Jones do? It's hard to imagine him supporting LIV.

"Noise is the second largest environmental cause of health problems after air pollution, according to the World Health Organization," Charlie Roscoe of the Harvard School of Public Health said. "It's been linked with issues ranging from sleep disturbance to poor concentration to risk of metabolic and cardiovascular disease and dementia." American society has become frenetic, with more noise that we now accept as the norm. Perhaps we can learn from other cultures that value a quieter environment. In Finland, silence is a sign of calmness and politeness, even when in someone's company for an extended period of time. The Chinese have an ancient proverb that there is "no wisdom like silence." Tokyo is 70 percent larger than New York City, yet one rarely hears a taxi or car honk its horn. Cell phones aren't used on trains or planes; even using them outdoors in a public space is looked down on.

Serenity and quiet are also becoming a luxury enjoyed by the rich, who can escape cities and noisy neighborhoods to find peace. Think of the bubble environments I mentioned earlier. Those in Bel-Air and the Montecito section of Santa Barbara enjoy a quieter, less stressful life than those who can't escape the commotion of modern life. The Masters has created an environment where both golden rules are followed. Not only do they treat people like they would like to be treated, but they also follow the ancient Egyptian proverb, "Silence is golden." It's one of the reasons we love it. Ryan Fitzpatrick, the Harvard-educated former NFL quarterback with a mountain-man beard, describes the Masters as having a purity to it. He rightly notes, "Taking away the cell phone is one of the big joys for a lot of people."

The Masters breaks the cycle and slows life down, allowing a patron to take it all in at a different speed. Multiply it by 40,000 other patrons doing the same and it creates a unique environment. Strangers say hello to one another. Smiles abound. There's a whole lot of contentment on those 365 acres.

Hootie Johnson started the cell phone ban. Billy Payne was chairman when the iPhone was launched, and he held the line: "I just don't think it is appropriate, the noise is an irritation." His successor, chairman Ridley, threw out the "if ever" card: "I don't believe that's a policy that anyone should expect is going to change in the near future, *if ever.*" My sense is that the tradition has become ingrained and is universally applauded. The "if ever" really means "never."

It's not difficult to imagine a future where unwanted noise intrusions get worse. Three likely scenarios that would further degrade our peace are noted below.

I'm firmly on the side of the union that represents flight attendants in opposing the use of cell phones in flight. I know the technology exists, but as we've seen from the example set by the Masters, using technology wisely is an art. The reality is that people don't know how to observe proper etiquette, and the flying experience is already bad enough. I'm sure the airline bosses will push for it because, like credit cards, it's another avenue for revenue. But creating the inevitable inflight fistfights caused by bad behavior is not something we need.

Ubiquitous drones are another possible downgrade. The revenue mongers at Amazon are pushing for approval so deliveries can be made via drone. It would represent another layer of undesirable noise pollution. The instant gratification world has already gone too far, and it's time we put the brakes on. Aside from critical medical supplies, nothing is so urgent that it has to be delivered by drone. We'll all have to wait for our Jergens Hand Lotion and Sponge Bob stickers to be delivered the next day. I prefer to hear birds chirping instead of drone engines whirring.

Finally, flying taxis are a stupid idea for the same reason. Yes, I've read about how quiet they'll be, but I also remember how Ford said the exploding-gas-tank Pinto was safe and how Philip Morris assured us that cigarettes didn't do harm. Not everything new is good, and not everything old is bad. Let's keep the skies as one of the few peaceful bastions.

Having discretion is also an important piece of Augusta National's ethos, and one of the reasons the Masters is incomparable. Not revealing everything creates mystique. As is their right, the club requires employees, caddies, consultants, and contractors to sign non-disclosure agreements, and all are prohibited from speaking publicly about the club. Curt Sampson obtained an (undated) Annual Report to Members, and it said, "The club wants no publicity except with respect to the Masters Tournament. Our members wish to enjoy the seclusion of a private club and prefer their visits at the club not to be publicized . . . It is expected that [members] shall actively discourage any form of publicity pertaining to the club, about which they have advance knowledge, if it is unrelated to the tournament—and especially if it is to be commercial in form." People who don't approve of Augusta National cite this and are aghast that they would do such a thing. They need to get over it. Every employer I worked for made me sign a non-disclosure agreement. Apple and Coke are also famously secretive companies, and rather than hurting them, it has enhanced their reputations.

People often confuse two concepts when they say Augusta National is overly secretive. They aren't, they are just using good discretion. Having discretion is different than being secretive. The club reveals quite a bit about its inner workings on its various social media channels. Having discretion means behaving in a manner befitting one's place in the world and having tact. Discretion also means behaving in a way that doesn't cause embarrassment and acting with a sense of decorum. It includes respecting others' rights to privacy and taking care in the way you communicate.

Charles Price wrote about Bobby Jones, "His public utterances were models of restraint and decorum. When Jones spoke, in public, or in private, his thoughts were measured, his words selected, his tone of voice modulated."

In a world awash with reality television shows and social media stars tripping over each other to see who can embarrass themselves more, the Masters remains a model of discretion and something we should seek to emulate. Like many of those highlighted so far, the primary lesson of the seventh principle is that less is more.

## Lessons from Augusta National Members

"I suggest that we all chill and develop a greater sense of civility, respect, and patience with each other" – Pete Coors, former chairman, Molson Coors Brewing Company

# How to Cultivate Civility

The foundation of the civility at the Masters is based on the calm environment they have created. Some companies have begun to recognize and embrace the idea that reducing noise and creating a calmer environment is good. Costco and the discount supermarket chain ALDI play no music in their stores, and I think it creates a better environment. (Both do so for the same reason—to avoid paying licensing fees so they can pass along lower prices to their customers). Picking a music genre—which primarily seems to be bad pop or bad rock—is like talking about politics. Regardless of what is played, half the customers won't like it. Better to turn it down, or make it something soothing, rather than a big thumping beat played loudly.

Walmart recently introduced "sensory-friendly hours" in their stores from 8:00 a.m. to 10:00 a.m., with dimmer lighting and no music. The company took the step so that those with sensory disabilities can shop in a less stimulating environment. Although the step is aimed at those with special needs, it provides a calmer environment for all shoppers and could be adopted more widely. Qatar Airways, Qantas, and Etihad Airways play calm music during boarding, creating a spa-like feel, rather than the high-volume, stress-inducing music most American airlines prefer.

Civility begins with lowering the noise level. The thought leader in cultivating a more civilized work environment and being more productive is a small firm based in Southern Pines, North Carolina.

## The Quiet Workplace

The Quiet Workplace is a consulting firm run by Joseph McCormack, specializing in helping companies improve employee performance by focusing on quieter work environments. His firm's approach is refreshing in a world awash with noise: "When we go to work, we often think that talking is a sign of productivity. We default to talk-to-talk and create non-stop noise. Work is about thinking and doing. We need to give ourselves a time and a place to work. And that means we need to introduce quiet into the workplace." His book, *Quiet Works: Making Silence the Secret Ingredient of the Workday*, describes the techniques used to set aside time each day to "focus, plan, do deep work, and make smart decisions." McCormack outlines a set of principles in his book to help people be more productive. One is to block out calendar time so no one can send a meeting planner or schedule a call. He advocates saying, "no, not now" more often while in a state of concentration, which is an effective technique to put off the increasingly large number of people who believe their current issue is the most critical priority. He also recommends taking technology timeouts, which I have always done and found effective.

Many people get sucked into responding to every text, email, Slack or Teams message immediately. The result is instantly gratifying but leads to low productivity. McCormack recommends setting up specific periods where you turn the volume off on your computer, silence your phone, and stop email and social media alerts to create an environment where more work can get done. He also advocates for something I've done for years. Putting up a "do not disturb" sign when working on something important. Some people might be put off by it, but it is a real productivity enhancer.

The pendulum between quiet workplaces and those that are chaotic has recently swung too far in the wrong direction. When Capital One built its new headquarters in Virginia, it used an open floor plan configuration, with phone booth areas set aside for those who want to get away from the din of other people talking, copy machines running, phones ringing, and people chatting near all the free snacks. Those who want to work in peace have to scurry around to find empty phone booths, or wear headphones. The pendulum has swung from having buildings full of offices to the other extreme—crazy setups with foosball tables and cafeteria-style seating.

When Adobe built its Founders Tower at its headquarters in San Jose, it designed "adventure rooms," including a virtual-reality room, a craft room, and a music room. To offset all the whimsy, the building also included "diverse spaces for employees to relax and recharge, including an outdoor terrace, wellness room, meditation room, and a library for deep focus and quiet space." The architectural firm that designed the building, Gensler, called it "the future of work." I hope not. Not everything new is good, and not everything old is bad. I'm traditional and believe it is easier to get work done in a tranquil environment with offices, without the need to pander to the whim of every prima donna in the organization with all these play spaces.

## Warby Parker

The eyewear company Warby Parker has a strong culture that helps it promote a more civil work environment. One of their core values is to "Treat others as they want to be treated," which includes designing products with empathy and having a positive attitude. Another is to "presume positive intent." Presuming positive intent is a powerful dynamic that reverses how we interact with others. Assuming positive intent is unnatural because our brains are hardwired to assume the opposite. This held us in good stead from being eaten by predators while in the wild. There's not much benefit in assuming positive intent from that lion standing nearby. It's not such a positive trait when interacting with a co-worker.

Typically, when someone offers criticism, we take it as a personal attack and assume they have another motive. Assuming that the person offering criticism has positive intent requires taking what they say at face value, ie, that they are offering criticism with a common goal of making a product or a project better, rather than trying to put the other person down. Assuming positive intent is a better way to interact with people—presuming they are fair, honest, and reasonable until they prove otherwise.

It is worth returning briefly to Pixar Animation Studios. They are clearly noteworthy for the quality of the films they produce. What is less well understood is that their continued success is the product of a culture that nurtures collaboration in an environment that prizes civility. Their success is not the result of relying on a "genius" model to generate ideas; rather, it comes from a system that values input from a variety of sources, and one that treats all team members as equals. The company describes what they do as a team sport where "everybody helped and even rescued the other."

### Lessons from Augusta National Members

"It's not about you. It's not about me. It's about us." – Lou Holtz, former head football coach, Notre Dame

# CHAPTER NINETEEN

# Principle #8

# Be Generous

Her death was imminent. That was the grim prognosis for the wife of one of Augusta National's golf professionals in 1970. When Clifford Roberts learned about how dire her condition was, he asked one of club's well-to-do members if his plane—modified so she could be transported lying down—could be used to fly her to a specialist, accompanied by a nurse.

The couple had a three-week-old baby and a toddler at home.

The heartbreak would be immeasurable.

She was flown to Boston and underwent a delicate operation. Followed by a week in intensive care. And another sixty days in the hospital. She had to return several months later for a second operation.

She survived by the generosity of an automobile tycoon. And a man described as a cold autocrat.

After learning that the couple was saddled with a tidal wave of medical bills and child-care costs, Roberts asked the members for donations. All expenses were paid.

Recency bias fools us into thinking that Augusta National and the Masters have always had deep pockets. In reality, the Masters got off to a shaky start, and its success was far from guaranteed. Roberts spoke about how the financial results of the inaugural 1934 tournament were disastrous, a trend that continued until after the Second World War. Donations had to be solicited among the club's wealthy members to fund the prize money. Generosity among the founding members would be among the club's enduring principles, which continues to this day.

In an interview in 2002, Hootie Johnson said, "The membership does not benefit from the tournament. The money goes back into the tournament, or we give it away." In keeping with their behavior of exercising discretion when it's appropriate, it isn't easy to discern how charitable Augusta National is, because until recently, they haven't talked about it. Johnson was the first chairman to go public regarding the club's generosity, with more than $25 million in charitable donations on his watch. After digging into various historical and current sources and relying on the *Augusta Chronicle's* extensive archives, there is evidence of the club giving away more than $175 million cumulatively. The total excludes small grants, so the actual number is higher. (The complete list of gifting is provided in the appendix.)

At the annual chairman's press conference, a frequent topic is the club's mission to grow the game, and they are putting money behind their words. Their giving shows unequivocally how much the club is spending to help grow the game in Asia and Latin America—$65 million to date, with large multi-million-dollar contributions each of the last several years. The Drive, Chip & Putt and Augusta National

Women's Amateur are also serious ventures, as indicated by the large amount of money the club is putting behind them. The club has given over $37 million to charities close to home, with the most significant chunk going to their local community foundation.

Unlike some other principles, this principle *is* embraced by many organizations. It is a necessary part of Augusta National's special formula, but they are not alone in their generosity. Giving back to communities and those less fortunate has always been a part of professional golf. The PGA Tour is proud of its giving: "The PGA Tour assists approximately 3,000 charities each year. Virtually all tournaments are organized as non-profit organizations to maximize charitable giving, and to date, tournaments across all tours have generated more than $3.37 billion." *Virtually* all tournaments, but not the Masters.

The Masters is not part of the PGA Tour, but a privately run invitational tournament. Augusta National is organized in corporate form, and not as a non-profit. It has been speculated that this is because there is less disclosure required, and because it brings less scrutiny from the IRS than if they were a non-profit.

Surprisingly, Augusta had been criticized on and off for its lack of charitable giving. Some historical perspective is helpful. In 1983, chairman Hardin noted, "First of all our objective is not to make money. Our objective is not to lose money. This is a pretty tight ship we have to run here because we want to minimize the commercial aspects. The National's members pay substantial dues for the privilege of belonging." This is a radical departure from the Augusta National of today, where both initiation fees and dues are low relative to the club's prestige. Taken at face value, his statement indicates that there wasn't necessarily a lot of money to give, which is believable, given the lack of revenue from their agreements with their U.S. broadcast partners.

Unlike the agreements with CBS and ESPN, the Masters gets broadcast-rights fees from partners outside the U.S., which began in earnest in the late '60s and '70s. The growth in merchandising operations beginning in 1990 also started to swell the coffers, leading to substantial revenue growth since Hardin spoke in 1983. The club does not disclose its finances, so there is no certainty about why they have been more benevolent over the last two decades. However, the growth of global broadcasting fees and increased sales from the larger golf shops would be large contributors.

Separate from Augusta National Golf Club, a non-profit entity was established in 2011, the Masters Tournament Foundation, as a vehicle to give money away. Chairman Payne announced the formation of the foundation: "The establishment of the Masters Tournament Foundation is central to fulfilling our responsibility of supporting the game's continuous growth around the world. This tradition, shaped by our founders Bobby Jones and Clifford Roberts, is the cornerstone of the Foundation's important commitment."

Between its inception and 2023, the Masters Foundation had inflows of $223 million and has made grants totaling $127 million. Between the foundation and Augusta National's direct gifts, total charitable grants exceed $175 million cumulatively. As of the last publicly reported information released by the IRS in 2023, the foundation had total assets of $81.7 million. The foundation has taken in an average of $18.1 million in new contributions each of the last five years. Thus, they are poised to continue to give generously into the future.

Although Augusta National, like all clubs, doesn't publish its membership rolls, the IRS requires charitable foundations to disclose who their board members are. It reveals a powerhouse of a governing board and is worth exploring in greater detail because it gives insights into the power structure within the club. Its eleven members are listed below:

1. Taylor Glover, Atlanta
   President and CEO of the foundation.
   Co-chairman of Turner Enterprises, the family office for Ted Turner.

2. Robert L. Johnston, Atlanta
   Secretary and treasurer of the foundation.
   Former executive vice president, Property Management /Co-Founder, Centennial Holding Co.
   Founder and chairman, First Communities.

3. Fred Ridley, Tampa
   The most powerful man in golf. Chairman of Augusta National, former president of the USGA, and former U.S. Amateur champion. Partner at Foley & Lardner LLP, specializing in real estate law.

4. W. Patrick Battle, Atlanta
   Managing Partner of Stillwater Family Holdings and former chairman of IMG College. Board member of MasterCraft Boat Holdings, Inc. and Acuity Brands.

5. Craig Heatley, New Zealand
   Serial entrepreneur and founder of Sky Network Television based in Auckland.

6.   Edward Herlihy, New York
       Co-chairman of the Executive Committee and partner at the law
       firm Wachtell, Lipton, Rosen & Katz; former chairman of the
       PGA Tour policy board.

7.   Terence F. McGuirk, Atlanta
       Chairman and CEO of the Atlanta Braves and member of the
       MLB Executive Council.

8.   Brian Roberts, Philadelphia
       Chairman and CEO of Comcast Corporation.

9.   Lee J. Styslinger III, Birmingham
       Co-chairman at Altec Inc. Serves on the board of the Harvard
       Business School, Workday, Vulcan Materials, and Regions
       Financial.

10.   Thomas C. Nelson, Charlotte
       Chairman, CEO, and president of National Gypsum. Member of
       the Business Council, the Business Roundtable, and the Council
       on Foreign Relations.

11.   Kessel D. Stelling, Jr., Atlanta
       Retired chairman and CEO of Synovus Financial Corp.
       Chairman of the Board of Regents of the University System of
       Georgia.

Imagine a vacancy and their advertisement to recruit a new
board member:

> Help Wanted: Captain of Industry, preferably
> someone with experience as a chairman, partner, or
> founder of a large and complex business. Membership
> on multiple boards is strongly desired. The candidate
> should have experience in philanthropy. We are
> partial to those living in the South who look good in

green. Your compensation will be commensurate with our other board members: zero.

Although I am making light of them, there is nothing humorous about what they are doing. They are to be applauded, not ridiculed.

In addition to writing checks to support its philanthropic efforts, Augusta National has a strong history of giving back to our servicemen and women. When the Second World War broke out, Bobby Jones volunteered at age forty and served as a captain in the Army Air Corps. He landed in Normandy the day after D-Day. Fort Eisenhower—previously Fort Gordon—is located twenty minutes from Augusta National, and the club has a long history of inviting soldiers to attend the Masters, starting with the servicemen's badge. Immediately after the war, the club allowed soldiers to play the course (in uniform), accompanied by Women's Army Auxiliary Corps members, also dressed in uniforms. Base personnel are still invited to the Masters each year, with one hundred badges given to the installation.

Some take a negative view of Augusta National and charge it with being elitist, exclusionary, and overly secretive. Augusta National could also be called the CEO Golf Club, because many of its members are highly successful business people. More accurately, they could be called the Charitable Giving Golf Club. Think about the members' wealth and how much money they give away each year. Warren Buffett and Bill Gates are prominent examples. The Gates Foundation (which Buffett has donated most of his wealth to) has $67 billion in assets and gives away more than $8 billion a year. Darla

Moore, a former partner in an investment firm, has a foundation with $500 million in assets that gives more than $15 million per year. Jeff Knox, a member who lives in the Augusta area, has a foundation worth $86 million and gives away between $3 and $4 million each year. These are just four members out of three hundred. You can do the math and calculate how much more is going on. Augusta National is as good a model as any when looking at how to be philanthropic.

One of the unwritten laws of economics is that wealth begets wealth. Money is not something Augusta National needs, so it has become a money magnet. For over one hundred years, the club has had some of the sharpest minds in business working to refine their principles. They run the best sporting event in the world. Herbert Warren Wind notes with his usual insightfulness that "it works more diligently than any other sports event not to overlook anything, however tangential or trivial, that can add to the pleasure of the occasion."
By doing so and treating people fairly, money flows into their coffers. Businesses and golf tournaments that have the balance wrong get the opposite. Customers aren't stupid. They can feel that they are being milked, which has a corrosive impact. The rich members of Augusta National don't need to get richer. Instead, they use the money raised from the Masters to do good. Helping others.

And it all started with a cold autocrat, who, it turns out, had a warm and generous heart.

# CHAPTER TWENTY

# Being Generous

Giving back to the game of golf, and to charitable causes generally, is an increasingly important part of the Masters story. There are other examples across the business world, in a variety of industries, where philanthropy is a core part of an organization's makeup. Three are noted below to illustrate that the Masters model can be paralleled and not diminish an institution's core mission. Quite the opposite, being generous enhances an institution's reputation.

## Salesforce

The San Francisco-based software company Salesforce has a noteworthy philanthropic focus, with the company espousing, "Give until it hurts. When the company was founded twenty-five years ago, we committed to giving back 1 percent of our time, 1 percent of our equity, and 1 percent of our product to support our communities. We call this commitment our one-one-one philanthropic model — and it's driven incredible impact to date: $728 million all-time giving in grants since our founding; 9.1 million volunteer hours from Salesforce employees worldwide; 59,000 nonprofits and schools using free and discounted technology." What makes Salesforce noteworthy is the depth of their commitment and how ingrained it is in their culture, a principle laid down by the company founder, Marc Benioff.

## Novo Nordisk

Companies based in Denmark engage in a different form of capitalism. Even public companies with shareholders are deeply charitable entities at their core. Novo Nordisk, based outside of Copenhagen, has a long history of developing drugs to treat diabetes. Of late, the company has been distinctly successful with a new class of drugs that help people lose weight, led by Ozempic and Wegovy. Many large Danish companies are majority owned by charitable foundations, and Novo Nordisk is no exception. Their foundation is worth $94 billion, making it the wealthiest charitable foundation globally, surpassing even the Gates Foundation in size. Between 2010 and 2015, the foundation distributed over $2.5 billion in grants. Novo Nordisk represents the opposite of the Friedman Doctrine and takes a balanced approach to shareholders, employees, and customers. They provide insulin at cost to large parts of the world whose populations cannot afford the drug.

Their "socialist" approach is different than that of the American system of capitalism since Denmark operates a welfare state. Their system has not hurt their business, nor their shareholders. Their stock has handily outperformed an index of the five hundred largest companies in the U.S.

The company also embraces the principle of continuous improvement, and it is so important to them that it is written into their company charter.

## H-E-B

H-E-B started as a small grocery store—founded in 1905 by a veteran—in the Texas Hill Country. Today, H-E-B is still family-owned and has three hundred stores throughout Texas. Like Buc-ee's, it has a cult following. In a 2022 Axios-Harris poll, which gauged the reputation of brands nationwide, H-E-B ranked number one in citizenship and trust and ranked number two overall. The company is also ranked third on the *Forbes* All-Star list. Supporting the community is a major part of H-E-B's identity and one of the reasons shoppers love it. Texas is home to a disproportionate number of military installations (fifteen in total), and H-E-B chooses to focus its giving efforts there. They have a program they call "Operation Appreciation," which they describe as "a pledge to honor the service and sacrifice of our active-duty service members, veterans, and their families, both in Texas and wherever they may be stationed worldwide." Since it was established less than a decade ago, they have given $12 million in support and hired 27,000 veterans. They have also donated forty-seven specially adapted homes to seriously injured veterans. The company also regularly sends care packages to military service members serving our country abroad.

Philanthropy from an individual point of view can take many forms, and it should be emphasized that being generous is not just about giving money. There are countless ways to be charitable—giving your seat to someone older than you is charitable; letting a car merge in front of you instead of trying to inch ahead of them is charitable; donating blood is an act of charity.

When I was quarantined in the hospital for a month undergoing my bone marrow transplant, there were musicians who would volunteer their time to come to the oncology floor and play, helping to lift others who were not having the best days of their lives.

It had a very positive impact.

The "pay it forward" movement was founded to create a ripple effect from acts of kindness. The simplest example is paying for the order of the person behind you at a drive-through. It's a small act of generosity that makes someone's day and changes perspectives about how much good there is in the world. It is the opposite of a transactional mindset, which focuses on calculating what we can get in return before helping someone.

Matthew Kelly, the author of *The Generosity Habit*, recommends giving something away every day: "It doesn't need to be money or material things. It could be complimenting a stranger, teaching someone how to do something, spreading a positive message, helping someone who is in a hurry, or simply smiling at someone generously." Most of us don't have millions of dollars to give like the Masters, but an important lesson is to broaden our definition of what giving back means.

## Lessons from Augusta National Members

"I know of no better human being on the planet than Tom Cousins. He walks in the shoes of those who are less fortunate and then takes action based on those experiences to change and improve their lives." – Former U.S. Senator Sam Nunn speaking about fellow Augusta National member Tom Cousins.

# CHAPTER TWENTY-ONE

# Principle #9

# Respect Tradition and Honor the Past

Tradition is an integral part of all sports and one of the reasons we find them appealing. Football has Gatorade showers, tailgating, Thanksgiving Day games, and the Lambeau Leap. Baseball has ceremonial first pitches, old-timers' day, curtain calls, pitcher's revenge, manager tirades, and the seventh inning stretch. The NHL has playoff beards, playoff handshakes, hat-trick hat throwing, and the Winter Classic. I appreciate all of them, but nobody does tradition and honors its past more than the Masters.

We tune in or go to the tournament because their traditions are comforting, like visiting a favorite elderly aunt. It starts with their iconic images, phrases, and traditions: Magnolia Lane, Amen Corner, the Green Jacket, the Green Jacket ceremony, pimento cheese sandwiches, the white caddie coveralls, the Par 3 Contest, the green folding chairs, the Champions Dinner, the "Augusta" theme song, "A tradition unlike any other," and "patrons." The leadership at Augusta National doesn't sit in their high perches deciding what new traditions to institute. Traditions have to grow naturally. Quirkiness is an underrated part of the club's heredity. Once a new routine has been established, they are stubborn about changing it, allowing it to grow organically into a tradition.

Beyond the well-known traditions, their lesser-hyped customs are equally appealing and endearing. Most golf tournaments begin with the prosaic. The Ryder Cup announces play by saying simply, "On the tee…" The British Open starts with, "This is game number …" And the U.S. Open is the most serious of the lot with, "This is the 8:45 a.m. starting time." Boring! The Masters starts a player's round with some panache. "Fore Please. . . Now driving …" was a tradition started by Augusta National member Phil Harison, Sr. in 1948. Harison was born in Augusta, growing up in a mansion behind the first green; he learned the game from a young age and became a member of Augusta National at the tender age of twenty-one in 1946. He was assigned as the chairman of the Starter and Pairings Committee the next year.

A quirky tradition can be found on a white table at the back of the tee box. The table contains scorecards, pencils, and a stack of pin location sheets held down by a brown rock. In the 1950s, Phil Sr. and his brother Gummy were the starters on a blustery day, and the papers kept blowing away. Gummy ran down to Rae's Creek and pulled out some rocks, which have been used on the starter's table ever since.

Harison Sr. died in 2008 after serving as the starter for sixty years. He witnessed every Masters tournament since its inception, beginning when he was eight. That's tradition. (The Harison family has been woven into the fabric of the club, with at least one family member, and often more, enjoying membership in the club, a tradition that continues today.)

Honorary starters are another tradition unique to the Masters. At the behest of Bobby Jones, Francis Ouimet, the 1913 U.S. Open champion, accompanied by Walter Hagen, became the first unofficial honorary starters in 1941. They were called the "grand old men," aged forty-seven and forty-eight, respectively, and played only nine holes. The honorary starter role officially began in 1963, when two Scotsmen were asked to lead off the tournament. Jock Hutchison, a native of St. Andrews, was a two-time major winner. Fred McLeod was born in North Berwick and won the 1908 U.S. Open at the Myopia Hunt Club. The two accomplished golfers were natural choices, each having won tournaments at Augusta National. The club hosted the first two PGA Senior Championships in 1937 and 1938—Hutchison won the inaugural event and McLeod, the second.

Hutchison served in the role until 1973, when he was eighty-eight. After Hutchison bowed out, the five-foot-four-inch McLeod served alone for three years, doing the honors until 1976. Both dapper dressers, they were tough old birds and wouldn't just hit ceremonial shots from the first tee, but would walk and play either nine or eighteen holes. During their latter years they walked with canes—McLeod doing so until he was ninety.

There was a four-year hiatus without honorary starters until 1981, when Byron Nelson and Gene Sarazen took over. Ken Venturi pinch-hit for one year in 1983, when Nelson was unavailable. Although Venturi had played in several Masters tournaments and won the U.S. Open, he said he had difficulty catching his breath before the shot because he was so nervous. Sam Snead made it a threesome beginning in 1984. After another brief hiatus without honorary starters, Arnold Palmer took on the role in 2007, serving alone until Jack Nicklaus joined him in 2010. The Big Three were reunited in 2012 when Gary Player joined.

To give some sense of how much of an honor serving in the role is, Palmer attended in 2016, in frail condition, even though he could not hit a tee shot. Although the Masters receives many accolades and is continually praised, nothing speaks to the reverence of the tournament more than the will exhibited by honorary starters to continue returning. Augusta National and the Masters are so fabled that the game's legends muster the energy to return just one more time. The honorary starter role is often one of the last deeds taken by each man before leaving us.

McLeod died one month after hitting his last tee shot at age ninety-four; Sarazen also died a month after his, at age ninety-seven; Snead died one month after his, at age eighty-nine. And Arnold Palmer died five months after his final appearance, at age eighty-seven. The Masters is so special, these legends don't want to, and can't admit that it will end someday. That is the ultimate expression of gratitude to a tournament that has meant so much to them and golf fans everywhere.

Lee Elder, the first Black man to play in the Masters, was invited as a special honorary starter in 2021, at age eighty-six. Elder wore a nasal cannula hooked up to an oxygen machine. Although he was unable to hit a shot, he stood from his chair on the tee—a proud man— raising his driver into the air to rousing applause from the patrons and former green jacket winners present. "It was so gratifying to be there, to have my family there with me, to see the journey I had been on, and to be at that particular point, and it was certainly one that we will never forget." Elder died seven months later, again demonstrating the will that golfers have to return to Augusta National just one more time. The honorary starters are a select club within the Masters, with only eleven esteemed golfers receiving the honor.

The Masters also shows respect to many groups beyond the honorary starters, allowing former champions to play in the tournament for life, and including them in the Par 3 Contest. Patrons especially appreciate the effort made by the older champs, who often receive standing ovations.

On the other end of the spectrum are the youngest players in the field, who are invited to engage in a time-honored tradition—staying in the Crow's Nest. The Crow's Nest occupies the third floor of the main clubhouse, just below the cupola, and during the Masters it serves as accommodations for the amateurs. Accessed by a steep stairway, there is a large framed black and white vintage photo of lifelong amateur Bobby Jones—sporting plus fours—at the top of the steps, a reminder of the high regard the tournament has for non-professionals.

The amateurs are also the guests of honor at a special dinner hosted by club members. It is a tradition dating back to 1948. Jones and Roberts would attend the dinners and give pep talks to the young contestants. The elegant white-tablecloth event is held in the Founders Dining Room, the table set with fine china, and next to each attendee is a picture of Jones standing in front of all four trophies from his Grand Slam feat. The dinner has always been popular and has swelled in size; in 2023, seventy-four members and dignitaries joined seven amateurs.

Aside from honoring golfers, the Masters continues to take an old-world approach to their tournament generally. The manually operated scoreboards are the best example, but also, the landline phones on the course that patrons can use remain an idiosyncratic tradition. Even the social media accounts incorporate honor and respect for past players.

The traditionalism of the club extends to how it works with outside entities. David Owen describes Cliff Roberts's feelings about the value of long-term relationships: "He believed in continuing relationships. He liked to use the same lawyers, bankers, photographers, doctors, suppliers, and contractors year after year." A thought process like his is increasingly disappearing in our transactional society, where the focus is on the bottom line. Owen continues, "The club has used the same bank since the 1930s. Clever lawyers could always find ways to wiggle out of contracts, and business relationships therefore needed to be founded on more than pieces of paper."

Suppose your organization was landlocked and was already chock-full of buildings on its campus; what would you do if you needed more space? You would dig underground and put in some new high-tech rooms. Of course you would. In 2021 the club created a "Green Jacket Vault." For titans lucky enough to receive the coveted invitation to join Augusta

National, the club doesn't pawn them off on an employee to get fitted for a green jacket. Instead, they have a special ritual. Of course they do. The club chairman escorts the blissful inductee into the back of the pro shop and opens an unmarked door leading down to the vault, where they meet a tailor to be custom fitted for their jacket.

The room that holds the roughly one hundred yet-to-be-assigned jackets is like something out of a Jason Bourne movie, accessed via a fingerprint scanner. Of course it is. The glass-fronted vault also holds one of the club's prized possessions—an early green jacket from the 1930s. The Green Jacket Vault is accompanied by another underground room, which they call the "Green Jacket Experience," and it has touchscreen displays that activate videos telling the story of the green jacket and how it evolved into a unique tradition.

Getting a green jacket is a cause for celebration, so there are two leather chairs as part of the Experience—with Augusta National logos on them. And there are two hidden liquor cabinets holding scotch and bourbon to toast the new member. Of course there are. In a club dripping with traditions, we would expect nothing less of Augusta National. It never ceases to amaze.

The reason the approach taken by the Masters resonates is because, as societal norms have changed, increasingly we don't respect tradition and honor the past. The political arena has become a cesspool where leaders no longer see value in respecting the work done by those who came before them. And the leaders take this approach because our society now values confrontation instead of compromise; rancor instead of civility. Imagine if Barack Obama had praised just one action George Bush took as valuable. Or if Donald Trump praised anything Obama did as valuable. The sky would fall. It's just not who we are anymore. *Everything* the opposite party does is bad.

The unintended byproduct of this environment is that honor has slowly been devalued, especially honoring the past. Although we still celebrate Veterans Day, Memorial Day, and the Fourth of July, they are widely seen as free vacation days. Most rarely give a second thought to what we are supposed to be honoring, and it's sad. When asked, "As far as you know, what does the term 'D-Day' refer to?" only 27 percent gave the correct answer.

If we don't even understand history, how are we going to honor the past?

Another reason the Masters remains a draw is that it is a constant in a world awash in change. Alexandra O'Laughlin of the Golf Channel describes the Masters as being closer to a holiday than a sporting event, which is a good comparison. It might not have turkey, mistletoe, or presents under the tree, but it is equally rich with tradition and an occasion to gather.

Change comes at us from all directions—rapid technological change, increasing urbanization, the rise of identity politics, the changing nature of society (especially the grievance and entitlement cultures), and the trend of increasingly large corporations driving smaller and boutique businesses out of business. There are fewer and fewer reliable things that we can look to year after year and decade after decade and think, *Ah, that's exactly as I remember it, with solid traditions and respect for the past.*

# CHAPTER TWENTY-TWO

# How to Respect Tradition and Honor the Past

It's a rarity today to find for-profit institutions that respect tradition to a great degree. America is a country focused on the future, not the past. That's not meant as a criticism; it's simply a reflection of who we are. There are exceptions. The Academy Awards offer lifetime achievement awards honoring past works and have an "In Memoriam" segment. Many universities and fraternal organizations also respect tradition and honor their pasts with elaborate rituals, although we're amateurs compared to how institutions in Great Britain uphold this principle.

## Wimbledon - The All England Lawn Tennis and Croquet Club (AELTC)

Wimbledon operates with four simple values: respect, excellence, integrity, and heritage. The first three are a part of many companies' value statements. You can even buy pre-made posters to hang in the break room extolling the virtues of each. Whether organizations live by them is another question. It is much rarer to see a value related to heritage.

Wimbledon aligns very closely to the Masters, with storied traditions—the all-white player dress code, the queue for day tickets, the well-behaved nature of the spectators, the tradition of remaining as non-commercial as possible, and the Royal Box. Their signature food and drink selections are memorable: freshly picked strawberries and cream and Pimm's. And we can't forget Rufus the Hawk.

AELTC also positions smartly dressed members of the British Armed Forces around the courts. The tradition began in 1946 when the championship resumed after the war. German bombs damaged Centre Court, and service personnel helped fans safely navigate a route to their seats. Today, more than four hundred members of all branches happily serve as unpaid volunteer stewards each year.

An inspiring tradition is the excerpt of Rudyard Kipling's poem, "If," written on the wall above the players' entrance to Centre Court: "If you can meet with Triumph and Disaster / and treat those two impostors just the same."

AELTC's attention to the small details is as noteworthy as Augusta National's—the perfect grass courts are vacuumed, painted, and hand-mopped every day before play starts. Sally Bolton, the CEO of Wimbledon, also embraces an ethos of continuous improvement: "Doing everything a little bit better every year." Wimbledon does an excellent job keeping commercialism tamped down as well. The television broadcast is pleasant to watch without the typical commercial onslaught. This is partly driven by the nature of the sport, with spectators able to watch uninterrupted coverage for fifteen to twenty minutes at a time, but also because of the club's principles. For a long time, there were no sponsor logos on the courts. Of late, they have permitted some discreet advertising on and around the court, although they are in the background. "Our clean court philosophy is at the heart of our brand," the commercial director for AELTC has said. Wimbledon takes it a step further and is vigilant about stamping out "ambush marketing," fans who are paid to carry items such as umbrellas or water bottles bearing heavily branded commercial messages. They temporarily confiscate them to keep the environment as commercial-free as possible.

Founded in 1868, AELTC also has a small and elite membership, with an even more restrictive admissions policy than Augusta National, limiting members to British citizens only. The standing joke is that the easiest way to gain membership is to win a Men's or Ladies' Singles Championship, although they are accorded honorary memberships only.

Attending finals matches (especially getting prime seating) is as hard as attending the Masters—the club issues debentures, giving holders an allocation of tickets for five years. The Centre Court debentures issued for the 2026-2030 tournaments sold for a lofty $150,000 per seat. Current debenture holders have the right to renew, and similar to Masters badge holders, they almost always do, leaving very few available for new fans. Aside from the debentures, AELTC offers reasonably priced tickets via a lottery, or fans can show up early and wait in line for tickets on "the queue," with enthusiasts camping out the night before.

Sticklers about their rules, umpires at Wimbledon are required to learn curse words in multiple languages, so if a player shouts them during a match, they can be fined. Even club members are not allowed to use Centre Court, which is exclusively used during Wimbledon.

Sir Ronnie Hampel, a member of Augusta National and AELTC, has helped the organizations share best practices, encouraging the leadership of both clubs to travel back and forth to learn from each other. The head groundsman of AELTC and the head greenkeeper of Augusta National visit each other's venues to learn best practices. When Berckmans Place was designed, it was modeled after Wimbledon's debenture hospitality areas. The organizations' technology strategies are similar, with AELTC likewise using IBM. Wimbledon's website and app are free of commercial clutter, easy to navigate, and chock-full of entertaining content.

The merchandising strategy of AELTC also mirrors Augusta National's approach. Daniel Ashmore, the head of Retail, Merchandise & Licensing for AELTC, spoke about their philosophy: "Our core values here include heritage and tradition, so it is really important to us to look backwards without being complacent and just trading off that." They have shifted their model over the last decade, doing most of their production in-house, so they retain more control. Ashmore continued, "I think our guiding principle in merchandise should be 'does it work on the court; does it work in the clubhouse?' And if it doesn't work in either of those areas, is it authentically something we should sell? If we wanted to just chase volume, then sure. But for the elements we are working with here at Wimbledon, it just doesn't make any sense at the Championships."

Wimbledon is widely watched around the world because it has maintained high standards. The tournament's philosophy is simple: "We always strive to do things as well as they can be done. With honor, integrity, and grace. A place where people value etiquette."

As much of the world has become homogenized, with cultures increasingly adopting similar conventions, ultimately, what makes Wimbledon stand out is an intangible quality. It has remained unabashedly English.

## British Royal Family

Although it has detractors, the British royal family is still held in high regard because it represents stability, legacy, and tradition. Crazy to compare a golf club to the monarchy? Not entirely, when you consider that they have *their* own golf club. The nine-hole Royal Household Golf Club, located in a private section of Windsor Great Park, was established in 1901 during the reign of Edward VII. While Augusta National is rich with tradition, few institutions honor traditions and the past more.

Who doesn't have just a tinge of awe watching the dazzling Gold State Coach roll down the Mall, pulled by the Windsor Greys, accompanied by a stirring rendition of God Save the King? The Brits are the masters of pomp, ceremony, and symbolism. The centuries-old tradition of the State Opening of Parliament is another prime example, dripping with pageantry, including a procession of Yeomen of the Guard walking two-by-two into the Palace of Westminster wearing their distinctive Tudor royal scarlet tunics, knee breeches, and black flat hats, carrying menacing partisan polearms. God Save the King indeed.

The parallels between the Masters and the royal family are striking. During formal dinners, employees from the "Master of the Household Department" use rulers to ensure that each piece of silverware and dinnerware is perfectly spaced. Videos of the Champions Dinner setup on the Masters website show the same attention to detail in the dining room and table setup. They're both insanely meticulous. The flower beds, lawns, and hedge rows at Buckingham Palace and Kensington Palace are as meticulously maintained as Augusta National. The @theroyalfamily Instagram account has 14 million followers and only classy content. The same is true of their Facebook account and website. As with everything they engage in, their use of technology is restrained. The royal family participates in over 2,000 public engagements annually, and more than 1,000 organizations have a royal family member as a patron. Aside from an occasional stray royal, what group of people has better manners than the king and his inner circle? They behave with the utmost discretion, revealing little about their inner workings.

On a side note, the royal family and Augusta National have two of the best wine cellars in the world, and it's undeniable that both relish in showing off their distinctive attire.

My experience is in the financial world, so I can speak most closely to the norms in that industry, but my sense is that it reflects how change plays out in many organizations. I have seen dozens of announcements in this tired form: "Jim has decided to pursue other interests and spend more time with his family. We thank him for his years of service and dedication to the firm and wish him well."

The reality is that Jim was pushed out because a new regime is in place, and they want to bring in their own people. Corporate America no longer says that people are pushed out or fired. Instead, they tell at best a half-truth, if not an outright falsehood: "pursuing other interests."

It's disingenuous, and companies aren't fooling anyone.

It's a good example of how much lawyers dictate corporate policies in our litigious world, and the logic is perverse: let's not say what really happened, for fear of being sued. Throughout the organization, from the most senior executives to the employees in the mail room, everyone knows what really happened. The problem with this sanitized version of the world is that it doesn't honor the past. Jim probably spent a decade or more killing himself for the company, missing sporting events for his kids, and getting home at midnight from delayed flights. Aside from this mealy-mouthed memo, Jim is accorded no respect. How about giving more credit where credit is due?

New leaders typically talk about themselves too much, focus on what was wrong with the past, and what they will do to fix it. That's human nature, but also a mistake. Leaders are more effective when they honor what their predecessors have done instead of just giving them lip service.

### Lessons from Augusta National Members

"The NFL is a part of the fabric of American culture, and we have a responsibility to honor that legacy." – Roger Goodell, commissioner of the NFL

# CHAPTER TWENTY-THREE

# Principle #10

# Use Scarcity to Create Value

Article I, Section 8 of the Constitution grants the power to print money to the federal government only. The rulers of Augusta National haven't read the fine print. Their golf shop prints money.

If you approached a bank asking for a loan and told them it would be used to start a retail store that would only be open seven days a year, you would be laughed out of the room. In the retail business, successful practitioners market their products, have a large footprint, and sell through multiple channels, including online. The Masters does none of the above. *Exceptio probat regulam.* That's Latin for "Augusta National has its own rules."

Anyone who has attended the Masters and witnessed the lines into the merchandise areas would be hard-pressed to argue that they haven't found the secret sauce of retailing, combining three special ingredients rarely found together. Denying buyers fifty-one weeks of the year creates scarcity and pent-up demand, and a carefully cultivated brand image makes being affiliated with the Masters desirable.

Those two elements are necessary, but not sufficient to achieve the kind of success the Masters enjoys. Quality is the final element. If their merchandise were sub-par, they wouldn't be the success story they are.

The golf shop experience typically begins with a wait, and often a long wait. Unlike lines at airport security or the supermarket, no one is moaning in these lines; patrons can't wait to see the merchandise spread. Copying a page from the Disney experience, patrons don't immediately enter the shopping area, but instead enter a series of corridors and wind through crowd control barriers until they are admitted in batches to prevent overcrowding. While waiting, a series of large screens keeps patrons entertained with videos and slide shows about the Masters, the Drive, Chip & Putt, and the Women's Amateur.

Once through the queue, patrons are greeted with a stylish environment to shop in—high ceilings, wide aisles, hardwood herringbone floors, dark paneled shelving, and natural light streaming in from skylights above. The look is Ralph Lauren, but patrons feel like they've been set loose in FAO Schwarz without the need to ask parental permission.

Seeing the store for the first time, the *Toronto Star* said, "The folks who run the Masters call it a golf shop. But it would more accurately be described as a Masters-themed superstore." The shop is spacious, twice as large as the congested shop it replaced, with 25 percent more employees. There are more mannequins than days of the year—385 human mannequins, plus one dog mannequin. Hats and T-shirts are the most popular items. Unsure of your preferred hat style? They've thought of everything: classic baseball-style hats, mesh-backed hats, bucket hats, large-brimmed hats, rope hats, toboggan hats, visor hats, retro-style hats, straw hats, and even a neon pink hat for kids—125 different styles. The shop sells a hat every second they are open.

So excited to attend the Masters, and unsure if they will ever return, patrons sometimes lose their senses. Jimmy Roberts interviewed a patron holding a large bag bulging with hats the year the new golf shop opened, asking why he bought twenty-seven hats. Looking somewhat dazed, his answer was, "What?" not because he didn't hear the question, but because he didn't think it was odd to buy so many. The only way to purchase merchandise at list price is in person at the Masters. Scarcity creates demand.

Although the Masters is famous for free parking and reasonable food prices, the largess does not extend to the golf shop. They are selling premium products and price them accordingly. This is not to say that they are overpriced; their prices are lower than British Open merchandise, and at the same level you would pay for merchandise from a good golf course or a pro sports franchise: T-shirts for $32, hats for $32.50, ball markers for $10, Tervis tumblers for $19, golf shirts for $89—or $110 for one made by Peter Millar. Some use their visit to finish Christmas shopping in April, others take it as an opportunity to buy a lifetime supply of Masters gear.

And then there are the resellers, primarily those who use eBay, who are buying thousands of dollars of items at a time. When the *Star* asked a cashier what the largest sale she had seen was, "Fifty thousand dollars" was her reply. "It was, basically, forty of everything." It wouldn't be surprising if the tournament cracked down on resellers at some point—like they do with those that resell badges—by limiting sales, since it cuts down on the exclusivity factor.

Another unique type of customer are the gnome shoppers. Kristi Boyd told the *Star*, "My daughter came last year and bought one, and it's worth a whole lot more now than it was then. It's one of those things, it's like a house. It goes up and up and up."

Shoppers with furry friends waiting at home can also indulge with a choice of pet collars, water bowls, dog bandanas, and leashes—all with the Masters logo on them. For those at the high end of the shopping spectrum, there are products tailored to their needs. The Masters has its own design studio and manufactures many of the products sold in the shop. They use cutting-edge computer design software to create artwork, signage, packaging, and their own patterns.

They also partner with upscale brands, handpicking only a few—MacKenzie-style lightweight Masters-branded carry bags ($995 new, $2,000 or more on eBay); Montblanc pens; Smathers & Branson hand-stitched needle-point belts; Tory Burch cashmere sweaters and cross-body bags; catstudio frosted drinking glasses; Martin Dingman leather goods; Maui Jim limited edition Masters sunglasses, and some special Masters Made in Italy items. Makers of products for the mass market dream of becoming a supplier to Walmart; likewise, high-end brands salivate at the idea of winning a mandate from the Masters.

By now, we know that the Masters thinks through every small detail, and the golf shop is no exception. Each year they pick a theme color for golf shop employees to dress in, and they all wear pastel-colored pullovers of the same shade. Spring has even arrived indoors! There are sixty-four registers, and the checkout process is efficient and friendly. Shelves are replenished as soon as they are cleared. After checkout, additional services are available. Those who don't want to carry their stash for the rest of the day can check it for free, or an efficient shipping station operation allows patrons to ship items home.

The sprawling merchandise operation we see today had humble beginnings. Merchandise at most golf courses is sold by the professional, who oversees keeping items in stock, and he or she keeps the profits. When it was a modest operation, the Masters also used the same model. Ed Dudley was the first professional at Augusta National, serving from the club's inception until 1957. During Dudley's tenure, he set up a small tent during Masters week and sold full sets of clubs, shirts, hats, and golf bags.

When Gene Stout succeeded Dudley as the head professional, patrons looking to buy Masters merchandise could do so from two facilities located in the parking lot—an open-air golf shop made of cinderblocks selling "sportswear and accessories," and two mobile office trailers hooked together selling "ladies' sportswear." A new golf shop inside the gates was built in 1990, although it was only a fraction of the size of the current building. It was expanded incrementally from time to time, but could not keep up with demand. In 2017, the new media building was completed, and the old one—adjacent to the golf shop—was torn down, finally creating the space needed for the large, spacious facility we know today, opening in 2018 to great fanfare.

The merchandising operation speaks to how loyal Masters patrons are, purchasing gobs of conceivably any product, as long as it has the yellow, red, and green logo on it. Ultimately, a brand is a promise, and the Masters has delivered on its promise for decades. Ritz-Carlton has been a brand success because no matter what location you visit around the world, the experience is of the same consistency and high quality. The Masters represents that same level of consistency and superior quality.

Like the best retailers, Augusta National uses sophisticated data analytics to project and optimize inventory levels and dedicate the most shelf space to the most popular products. The quality of their shelving layouts, display design, and product placement speaks to a high level of sophistication, as does the quality of the items they sell, upholding the brand's image. They have avoided the ugly duckling items that other major tournaments have offered. No one would accuse the Masters of setting trends; the traditional style prevails, with restrained use of colors.

Both the COVID-19 pandemic and the resultant spike in inflation have caused a dent in brand loyalty, with shoppers becoming more fickle, creating a willingness to try new brands and make substitutions to lower-priced products. Not at the Masters, where very little will seemingly keep patrons from filling their baskets. Buyers turn off the price sensitivity switch when they walk through the door. They feel lucky to have been admitted into the inner sanctum of golf shopping.

The Masters doesn't disclose how much money they make each year on their golf shop sales, although the most frequently cited number is a $69 million estimate by *Forbes*.

The *Forbes* estimate doesn't come with a description of its methodology, and it represents gross sales without factoring in the cost of the goods and the labor needed to sell them. The best way to determine whether the $69 million is higher than average for a sports event is to look at comparable events. *Forbes* estimates that Wimbledon makes $50 million from merchandise and concessions combined. On the surface, the Masters merchandise sales would compare favorably, particularly because Wimbledon sells merchandise online and the Masters doesn't.

Another way to look at the *Forbes* estimate is to determine how many patrons attend the Masters and assume an average amount spent per patron. During practice rounds, 50,000 patrons are admitted, and on tournament days the number is reduced to 40,000 to ease congestion. That makes 310,000 bodies traversing the property over a week, although many people attend on more than one day and seemingly don't drop a big wad daily. If we reduce the total number of patrons by half, accounting for people who attend on multiple days, we can assume there are 155,000 unique individuals attending. Each would have to spend an average of $445 to get to the *Forbes* estimate, which seems quite possible based on my experience seeing what the average patron buys. Buy two T-shirts, a hat for yourself and your regular foursome, a polo shirt, and a pullover, and you're at $445. The hats are the Masters equivalent of a razor and get patrons through the door. After that, they succumb to the allure of Masters merch and buy plenty of blades. Curt Sampson, writing in 1998, semi-facetiously described the Masters as the only sporting event that "costs $20 to get in and $200 to get out."

Results like this don't happen haphazardly. Although Augusta National runs the Masters through a series of committees made up of members, they also rely on full-time staff to do much of the heavy lifting, particularly in the area of merchandising. "Good artists copy, great artists steal," Pablo Picasso is known for saying. Augusta National's Chief Merchandise & Creative Services Officer was hired from Disney, where he served as a Director of Product Development & Design. It is no coincidence that the Masters's retail sales have exploded over the same time frame he has been with the club, roughly a dozen years.

The Masters serves as a learning experience for even the most accomplished practitioners. Greg Sankey, the chairman of the SEC football conference, mentioned how he walks around the tournament taking notes, trying to figure out what makes it different. Commenting on how the golf shop is organized and works, he said, "Think about how they present their sales to fans… how can we be more like this as a standard of excellence. Those learning experiences are real for me."

Disney runs a program called the Disney Institute, with executives and professionals attending training sessions to learn what is behind their special formula running the theme parks. It seems unlikely Augusta National will ever operate a training program about their merchandising operation, however, their formula for success can be summed up on a Post-it note: scarcity, brand reputation, and quality.

<br>

**Lessons from Augusta National Members**

"There is profit in scarcity." – T. Boone Pickens, Founder and chairman, Mesa Petroleum

# CHAPTER TWENTY-FOUR

# How to Use Scarcity to Create Value

Scarcity is an effective marketing strategy that can convert a tentative shopper or browser into a customer. At its most basic level, online retailers use the tactic often. Both Amazon and Etsy display a box if an item is low in stock with a message noting, "only two remaining," to entice buyers to act. Marriott and other hotel chains do the same when customers book online: "Only three rooms left at this price." Several years ago, Starbucks offered a pink-colored, "Unicorn Frappuccino for a limited time, while supplies last," and it created a craze, their stores overrun with traffic. Nike releases limited edition sneakers and does exclusive collaborations to create a sense of scarcity, with the items quickly selling out.

The Masters takes scarcity to a different level. It is the ultimate manifestation of scarcity marketing, although a French luxury retailer also excels at the practice.

## Hermès

Founded in 1837 in Paris, Hermès has been run by the same family for over six generations. Although it is a public company, the family still owns 70 percent of the shares, so they have the freedom to think long-term and make decisions accordingly. Their Birkin and Kelly bags are sought after by wealthy people the world over, with the company deliberately limiting production to maintain scarcity. "They have taken scarcity to a point that Birkin bags may as well be unicorns," Kurt Philip of the marketing firm Convertica says. He goes on, "You go to any one of their shops and you're told there's none available. You ask when they'll have it and they tell you they don't know. Now, do you think all these jumping through hoops stop people from buying a $10,000 bag? No! Quite the opposite. It fuels their desire for it." The waiting list for Birkin and Kelly bags stretched out for years, and, like Masters tickets, the backlog became so long that Hermès eliminated it, and now only sells the bags to its best customers.

Beyond using scarcity as a tactic, many aspects of how they manage their business mirror Augusta National's approach. Hermès doesn't advertise Birkin or Kelly bags, and like Costco and In-N-Out Burger, word of mouth is the primary way they spread the word. Discretion is another part of the Hermès mystique, with the family focused on maintaining not only the integrity of the craftsmanship but also the brand identity. Just as Augusta National doesn't reveal how many tickets it sells or how much it makes on its merchandise operation, Hermès likewise doesn't disclose how many Birkin bags are made each year.

The company is among the wisest users of social media across the web—their elegant Instagram account has over 14 million followers, and echoing the Masters, it is non-commercial in its approach, focusing instead on evocative imagery.

While the Masters is known for its green jacket, Hermès has an equally recognizable brand color—a distinctive, bold orange they use in their packaging. In Grand Rapids, Michigan, there is a company called Pantone that is the global keeper of colors, cataloging them so that when paint companies, designers, and such, are looking to match a color, there is a common standard. Crayola makes 148 crayon colors, but Pantone has 2,161 different variations. (Green jackets are Pantone 342.) Hermès takes it further than Augusta National and intentionally uses a color not in the Pantone catalogue. They have even tried to trademark it, which the European Union has refused to do, arguing that you can't own a color.

Mirroring the Masters, their brand transcends time and trends. Like those who go into the Masters golf shop and think nothing of spending $1,000, Hermès's customers are equally cost-insensitive. Ben Gilbert and David Rosenthal perfectly describe why people go crazy when they enter the Masters golf shop. On their *Acquired* podcast, they say, "When you buy Hermès, you're not just buying a luxury product. You're buying a feeling that connects you to the maker and the place that it was created. You're trying to buy a piece of Hermès's heritage and reputation and hoping to adopt it as part of you, as a part of your identity. You are seeking, whether it is conscious or not, to let other people know about this too, and you're not necessarily trying to signal it to everyone, but you do want to signal it to the right people who would appreciate it." Replace every instance of Hermès with the Masters, and it explains the frenzies in the golf shop. Nobody *needs* to buy a Masters branded Tory Burch bag; it's a total luxury. People are seeking the brand affiliation.

One final note, Hermès also has a very low employee turnover, only 6 percent per year. Why do I keep mentioning this since it has nothing to do with the Masters? It wasn't something I set out to do, but I found the commonality among all these great businesses compelling. By comparison, one-third of all jobs turn over in aggregate every year across all industries, to give a better sense of how astounding these companies are and how well they treat their associates. Low turnover appears to be closely correlated with companies that pursue more than profits at all costs.

# CHAPTER TWENTY-FIVE

# Themes and Observations

When looking across the ten principles there were several common themes that emerged, accompanied by some surprises.

## Japanese Parallels

One of the surprises that emerged when looking at how Augusta National approaches the Masters was the many parallels to Japan. Meticulousness and attention to detail are hallmarks of Japanese society; the wait-and-see approach as it relates to technology without the need to be a first-mover; the similarities to continuous improvement; the focus on civility; and how they manicure trees, shrubs, and plants. The bigger takeaway from this observation is how antithetical to current American societal norms many of the Masters principles are. Going against the grain has been successful for Augusta National, and it crystallizes a learning opportunity.

## Quirks and Charms

Another surprise was how quirky the club's decision-making has been, sometimes bordering on the irrational. The greenkeepers only rake the pine straw around the trees clockwise! They don't use an electric vacuum cleaner inside the clubhouse since the noise would disturb the reserved ambiance; instead, they use an old-school manual push-style carpet cleaner that makes no noise.

The *Los Angeles Times* reports how the food menu evolved: "No hot dogs or hamburgers are on the menu because members consider smoke from grills as being offensive." For a long time, the Masters didn't show the first nine holes on television. It wasn't until 1997 that they began to do so, long after demand for Masters tickets outstripped supply.

Being quirky is a virtue. Quirks add charm. Charm is captivating. Being captivated makes us yearn for more.

## Money is Not the Point

Augusta National could make significantly more money by charging broadcasters higher fees (or any fees at all in the United States). Or they could raise food prices and sell merchandise online. Lynsi Snyder talks about how some things are more important than lining the pockets of In-N-Out's owners, namely, maintaining a quality product. AELTC limits their merchandise selection only to products of the highest caliber, forgoing sales, rather than chasing volume. Hermès could sell more Birkin and Kelly bags if it ramped up production, but chooses not to. Costco management has coined a phrase, "the intelligent loss of sales," intentionally giving up some sales to achieve other goals. The fact that more businesses don't do it shows how deeply ingrained the profits-first mindset has become, with money outweighing all other considerations.

## Attention Spans, De-Stressing, and the Long View

Some tangential observations relate to how our society operates. We live in a time of instant gratification and short attention spans. The Masters flips the dynamic, primarily because we unplug and relax. It's easy to soak up whatever is in front of us. Time expands. As do attention spans.

In most of our quotidian lives, stress and incivility keep popping up, and they become a vicious cycle: a lack of rules can lead to disorder, which in turn leads to stress, which in turn leads to incivility. The rules the Masters have in place lead to more civility and less stress. They are worth emulating.

Augusta National moves cautiously. Having a time horizon of decades seems preposterous, but that is how the Masters operates. Their decision making is thoughtful and deliberate. It is not for tomorrow, but for the long term. It is a lost art.

## Restraint

Using restraint emerged as a common thread among many of the businesses highlighted. In-N-Out Burger, Apple, Costco, Wimbledon, and Hermès all use it to differentiate their brands. It's an underappreciated part of Augusta National's ethos.

## Talent Management

While it isn't possible to delve deeply into the talent management process behind the Masters without access to the club's leadership, it is clear they do an excellent job at it. They have the pick of the litter in terms of their ability to select broadcasters and writers who contribute to their website and app, and they pick the best. Their social media personnel are also best-in-class. The hiring of their Merchandise & Creative Services Officer from Disney is another obvious example, but the way they manage the tournament and train the personnel on-site for the week is nothing less than astonishing. The screening process they use to select only people who are merry and bright across every job has yielded an outsized benefit to the tournament. No doubt, the behaviors have something to do with being in an environment that is so inspiring. But having bathroom attendants and those working cash registers acting upbeat all day? C'mon. There's something else at work here that is difficult to articulate.

### Lessons from Augusta National Members

"I am here solely and singularly because I have the honor and privilege of leading an amazingly talented team of remarkable staff and loving friends. It is them, not me, who masterfully executed our recent plan to leverage the powerful brand of Augusta National and the Masters." - Billy Payne, speaking at his Hall of Fame induction ceremony.

## Expanding Your Market

Another underappreciated aspect of Augusta National's work is how it has instituted strategic initiatives to grow not only its audience but also the game of golf in general. Its substantial support of programs outside the traditional base demographic of golf is a clever way of approaching a long-term growth strategy. It is an important lesson in how to think laterally.

Golf's demographic traditionally skews toward older men (the median age of a PGA Tour television viewer is sixty-three). Rather than taking an incremental approach to growth within their existing demographic, the club went the opposite way. They focused on a demographic that is younger, more female, and located outside the U.S.

Their sponsorship of four new initiatives shows how they approached the problem smartly. Their Drive, Chip & Putt competition is focused on girls and boys aged seven to fifteen. The Augusta National Women's Amateur helps expand the game among young women. Kim Lewellen, the head coach of the Wake Forest University women's golf team, talks about how she has seen a rise in participation among young women because of the Women's Amateur, and directly attributes it to the fact that it is played at Augusta National. Justin Silverstein, the head golf coach at USC, describes it as a "huge platform" that attracts much more interest in the sport among young girls.

The club's involvement with the Latin American Amateur Championship is helping to grow the game in a critical emerging golf area, and their involvement in the Asia-Pacific Amateur Championship focuses on a high-growth market where 60 percent of the world's population lives. To support their substantial investment, the club has embraced TikTok, which makes sense since a large proportion of the platform's users live in Latin America and Asia, and are young.

## Pursuing Excellence

As one of the greatest events in the world, it's surprising that more entities don't operate using the same principles as Augusta National. Too many organizations settle for mediocrity. To replicate the magic of the Masters, a simple mindset is needed: a desire and commitment to pursue excellence. Disney makes the commitment, and wants kids to have a once-in-a-lifetime experience, so they pay attention to the smallest details and go out of their way to make people's day. It doesn't have to be any more complicated than that.

# CHAPTER TWENTY-SIX

# Why the Masters is So Meaningful

Every time I go to the tournament in person I leave with the same dream—I dream that the world could be more like the Masters. Reality sinks in when I arrive at the airport in Atlanta and the hard edges of our modern world assert themselves. The dream shatters into a million tiny pieces when we taxi to the runway and the credit card hard sell comes onto the video screen on the seatback. The principles provide the roadmap for improvement, if the approaches taken by the highlighted organizations were emulated more.

In response to one of the club's Instagram posts, a fan replied: "Best week of the year, and this year the tourney ends on my sixtieth birthday. Been watching since I was a little girl, with my dad. The flowers, the music, the course … everything. Dad now has dementia and is ninety-one, but when I watched a few holes with him on Thursday, he said 'are those azaleas?'"

That's what the Masters means.

Jim Nantz has a ritual he performs on Wednesday every year before the tournament starts. When the course is closed, he walks down to the twelfth green and says a prayer of gratitude for being there.

That's what the Masters means.

The golf writer Claire Rogers describes the day she spent at the Masters with her father and sister as the best day of her life.

That's what the Masters means.

Having founders who put the right culture and principles in place is a key part of Augusta National and the Masters, and their greatest asset. Bobby Jones is still the guiding spirit. An important part of the Masters appeal is that it is so reliably good, delivering a quality product year after year. Augusta National calls the Masters "the last non-commercialized sporting event in the world," which says a lot about where we find ourselves.

The pace of change has become so rapid that it is nice to have something that we can count on that remains true to its principles. It's no wonder we long for a time and a place before so many "innovations" occurred. How agreeable it is to find an institution that values civility, respects people, uses technology the right way, continually improves, is philanthropic, and that doesn't worship at the altar of the almighty dollar.

Far be it from me to give advice, but I have tried to embrace many of the things the Masters does right to better myself. I try to give back more, and not only financially. I stopped engaging with simpletons on social media and stopped watching news on cable television, and I am happier as a result. I try to make self-improvement a part of my ethos. I am a better version of myself when I put down my phone and engage more.

I have begun to seek out smaller producers that "get it" and care about the smallest details of their products. In the same way that Wimbledon is quintessential English and proud of it, the Masters is quintessential Southern and proud of it. We need more of that. The oversized tentacles of big business reach everywhere, often to the detriment of originality and local flair. I avoid the homogenization of strip malls filled with banks, a CVS, and chain stores, in favor of businesses with personality. Sameness is drab.

I find myself watching less and less commercialized sports on television and instead watch paid streaming services like Netflix without ads. I increasingly get news from less commercially oriented sources such as Substack newsletters, podcasts, and blogs.

I make sure I go out of my way to recognize the "hidden" people in our society, who deserve more respect. When I was undergoing my induction chemotherapy, I had a bad reaction to one of the nasty drugs they gave me. The hospital of the University of Pennsylvania has some of the best cancer doctors that exist, graduating from the best medical schools, and their research is cutting-edge. Their nurses are equally impressive. As my condition started to deteriorate, I was put on morphine to kill the pain (never a good sign), and I began to focus on the simplest of all human actions. Taking another breath. One of the night-shift nursing assistants—whose job is to take vital signs and change sheets—had seen other patients who had deteriorated previously, and she knew I was about to endure a trying time, although I didn't.

Before I was taken to intensive care, she sat next to my bed and held my hand, offering positive encouragement and her prayers.

Alana is her name, an angel from Trinidad.

She understood that despite all the fancy equipment and drugs and excellent doctors, it is important not to lose the human touch, and it meant so much. The compassion she showed reminded me how important it is to honor and respect everyone, and not only those who are the most visible, or successful, or within our own little sphere.

May God bless her loving soul.

As I was scraping bottom, with a dozen baffled doctors unable to fix my problem, I needed something to hold onto. When I hit my nadir, I prayed that I would get better so I could see my children grow up and be happy. I battled ceaselessly so I could live a long life with my loving wife. It sounds odd, but I also dreamed of returning to the Masters again.

I've lived two lives. The first was a life filled with joy and a level of success and happiness I never dreamed of. The second has been full of pain, non-stop medical care, disappointments, and setbacks.

Dreaming of a return visit to Augusta National was a way to return to my old life. I was trapped for a long time in the sanitized indoor environment of a hospital, overwhelmed by needle stick after needle stick, ceaselessly beeping monitors, soul-crushing fluorescent lighting, round-the-clock infusions, and injection after injection. It took a big toll. I don't know if long hospital stays can trigger PTSD, but I felt traumatized. When I was discharged after many complications and unexpected turns, I pestered my oncologist for permission to make the trip. She reluctantly agreed because she knew how much I loved golf. She didn't know much about the game, but as Tiger noted, she knew what the Masters was. Because my immune system was compromised, I couldn't fly, so we drove the seven hundred miles.

I lost my freedom and my dignity, but I intuitively knew what I needed. I wanted to get outside and breathe fresh air in my favorite spot. When I finally hobbled up the stairs and we sat in the grandstand overlooking the thirteenth green, my mental healing process began. I felt that I was once again alive.

That's what the Masters means to me.

Geoff Shackelford, a long-time golf journalist with high standards and an elegant and witty writing style, was the inspiration for this book. He has attended the Masters in person for decades, and writing in his Substack newsletter, the *Quadrilateral,* he sums up the magic formula Augusta National has put together: "Once again the Masters provided its annual reminder that'll fly over private equity heads: if you consistently treat your customers well, give them a good value, relentlessly search for ways to improve and invest in your facility, the customer will pay you back out of appreciation when sensing an entity is constantly striving for excellence. The Masters and its iconic logo means something special for simple reasons that so few businesses seem able to replicate. May it never change."

Amen.

"No one big dramatic thing has made the Masters the immense success it is every year . . . It is the sum of its tiny well-oiled parts . . . each one contributing, like a Swiss movement, to the marvel of synchronization that is the Masters." – Charles Price

# Appendix

**Detailed estimate of cumulative charitable giving
(excluding small grants)**

| | | |
|---|---|---:|
| Latin American Amateur Championship | $ | 32,754,644 |
| Asia-Pacific Amateur Championship | $ | 32,324,503 |
| Augusta National Women's Amateur | $ | 24,127,121 |
| Drive, Chip & Putt | $ | 22,285,242 |
| Community Foundation Central Savannah River Area | $ | 19,500,000 |
| World Golf Foundation | $ | 10,000,000 |
| Georgia Regents University Cancer Center | $ | 6,000,000 |
| Hurricane Helene Relief | $ | 5,000,000 |
| PGA Tour | $ | 3,000,000 |
| Japanese Tour | $ | 2,250,000 |
| COVID-19 Relief | $ | 2,000,000 |
| PGA European Tour | $ | 2,000,000 |
| First Tee of Augusta | $ | 1,880,000 |
| PGA Tour Foundation | $ | 1,300,000 |
| Charities Aid Foundation America | $ | 1,243,000 |
| Paine College Lee Elder Scholarship Foundation | $ | 1,200,000 |
| PGA Tour Charities | $ | 1,100,000 |
| USGA | $ | 1,100,000 |
| LPGA Foundation | $ | 1,000,000 |
| Augusta Technical College | $ | 1,000,000 |
| Bobby Jones Golf Course Foundation | $ | 1,000,000 |
| LPGA | $ | 1,000,000 |
| South African PGA | $ | 750,000 |
| PGA of Australia | $ | 750,000 |
| Annika Foundation | $ | 500,000 |
| Arnie's Army Foundation | $ | 250,000 |
| | | |
| Total | $ | 175,314,510 |

# **Notes**

Epigraph

1.  Fred Ridley, Chairman's news conference at Augusta National, April 9, 2025.

Chapter One

1.  No byline, Sport: Like Father, Like Fun, *Time*, May 12, 1941.
2.  John Boyette, Sportsmanship one of Jones' greatest gifts to the game, *Augusta Chronicle*, March 16, 2013. - Quote about honesty.
3.  Herbert Warren Wind, Robert Tyre Jones, Jr., *Following Through*, Ticknor & Fields, 1985. – Quote about Jones's qualities.
4.  https://bobbyjones.org/about-bobby-jones/history - Jones quote about priorities.
5.  Charles Price, *A Golf Story*, Triumph Books, 1986. – p. 161, quotes comparing Jones and Roberts.
6.  SI Staff, Calling the Shots: Amiable Autocrat Frank Chirkinian of CBS Is the Master of the Masters Telecast, *Sports Illustrated*, April 10, 1995. – Quote from CBS producer.
7.  Curt Sampson, *The Masters: Golf, Money and Power in Augusta, Georgia*, Villard, 1999. p. xxi.
8.  *1992 Masters Journal.* Sarazen quote. p. 8.
9.  Clifford Roberts, *The Story of Augusta National Golf Club*, 1978, Doubleday. p. 225.

Chapter Two

1.  Justin Teitelbaum, The Masters Tournament at Augusta Is Leaving $269 Million On the Putting Green, *Forbes*, April 7, 2022. – Sales estimates
2.  Kyle Porter, We Will Buy You Ryder Cup Tickets. *Normal Sport*, November 18, 2024. – Brand quote
3.  @themasters, *Instagram*, April 6, 2016.
4.  @themasters, Gnome – Day in the Life, *TikTok*, April 12, 2024.

Chapter Three

1.  Bill Fields, The Enveloping Beauty of Augusta National, *Masters.com*, April 5, 2015. – Palmer quote.
2.  Golf Digest, *YouTube*, Mar 30, 2016. - Gretzky and Ogilvy quotes.
3.  Brendan Porath, *The Masters and Its Patrons, The Fried Egg, April 8, 2024.*

Chapter Four

1. Peter Hartlaub, On 25th anniversary of Toy Story, a look at the film's surprising Bay Area birthplace, *San Francisco Chronicle*, December 9, 2020. – Quote on Pixar and background.
2. Mark Townsend, Best Masters Quotes in History, *Golf Monthly,* April 4, 2023. –Woods quote.

Chapter Five

1. *Sports Illustrated*, April 10, 1995. – Jones and Roberts comments.
2. Price. Quote about Roberts autocrat in the absolute. p. 215.
3. SI Staff, The Coverage Was Masterful, *Sports Illustrated*, April 23, 1984. – Longhurst quote.
4. Justin Williams, Chirkinian is remembered as pioneer of televised golf, *Augusta Chronicle*, April 6, 2011. – Quote from Wright.
5. Owen – Roberts quote to CBS, p. 200.
6. Ben Nicholson-Smith, Vin Scully always knew what to say, and when to say nothing at all, *Sportsnet.ca*, August 3, 2022.
7. Richard Goldstein, Frank Chirkinian, the Father of Televised Golf, Dies at 84, *The New York Times*, March 6, 2011. - Comment about epitaph.
8. James Colgan, Eye on history: A look at the evolution of CBS' Masters broadcast, *GOLF,* November 14, 2020.
9. Marika Washchyshyn, Broadcast Rules for the Masters Are as Strict as You Think, *GOLF*, July 14, 2015. – Thirty-three rules.
10. Meet the Press, June 1, 1986. – Schultz comment.

Chapter Six

1. Jim Collins, *Good to Great*, Collins Business, 2001.
2. Marketing Strategies and Marketing Mix of In-N-Out Burger, *The Brand Hopper*, September 3, 2013.
3. Lynsi Snyder, *The Ins-N-Outs of In-N-Out Burger*, Thomas Nelson, 2023. – Quotes p. xx.
4. In-N-Out-Burger customer loyalty based on Net Promoter Scores. https://www.comparably.com/brands.
5. Nick Hobson, There are Successful People and Really Successful People, *Inc.com*, March 21, 2023. – Buffet quote.

Chapter Seven

1.   Herbert Warren Wind, The Masters' 50th Anniversary, *Following Through*, Ticknor & Fields, 1985. p. 341

2.   No byline, A Brief History of Obsessive-Compulsive Disorder, *Kairos Wellness Collective Blog*, Undated.

3.   Ocduk.org, History of behaviors of Nikola Tesla and Howard Hughes.

4.   Owen - Details about Roberts personality quirks, p. 23.

5.   Walter Isaacson, The Real Leadership Lessons of Steve Jobs, *Harvard Business Review*, April 2012.

6.   No byline, Players Appreciate Augusta's Attention to Detail, *Masters.com*, April 8, 2024.

7.   Alex Myers, Confessions of a Masters gallery guard: "They've got more rules than. . . ", *Golf Digest*, April 6, 2016.

8.   Zac Rayson, Painted grass, banned words and $2 sandwiches: Inside the perfectly weird world of The Masters, *Foxsports.com.au*, April 16, 2024.

9.   Joe Boschetti, *Details in Architecture*, Images Publishing, 1999. – Mies quote.

10.  Bill Pennington, At Augusta National, If You Have to Ask the Answer is No, *New York Times*, April 14, 2013.

11.  Marco Margaritoff, The Inside Story Of Walt Disney's Secret Tunnels Beneath The Magic Kingdom, *All That's Interesting*, April 16, 2021.

12.  Brendan Porath, The Masters and Its Patrons, *The Fried Egg*, April 8, 2024. – underground tunnel system.

13.  Joell Beall, Augusta National completes tunnel to state-of-the-art compound ahead of 2020 Masters, *Golf Digest*, Feb 17, 2020.

14.  Jeff Williams, As a New Maintenance Facility Comes on Stream Nothing is Left to Chance, *Masters Journal*, 1994. – Motivational quote is from Jimmy Johnson.

15.  Augusta Anonymous: Superintendent secrets at The Masters, *Golf.com* YouTube channel.

16.  Charles F. Knight, *Performance Without Compromise*, Harvard Business School Press, 2005.

Chapter Eight

1.   Ritz-Carlton Leadership Institute, The Power of Empowerment, March 19, 2019.

2.   Joseph A Michelli, *The New Gold Standard*, McGraw Hill Books, 2008. – "Mystique" system, quote from Schulze.

3.   https://ritzcarltonleadershipcenter.com.

4.   Buc-ee's comments - *Yelp.com*.

5.   Alan Schwarz, Customer Experience All-Stars, *Forbes*, February 20, 2024.

6.   Larry Bossidy, *Execution: The Discipline of Getting Things Done*, Crown Currency, 2002.

## Chapter Nine

1. Peter Adams, 52 percent think there is too much advertising, *Marketingdive.com*, March 16, 2021.

2. No byline, Welcome to the ad-free Internet, *Economist,* December 16, 2023. - Madison and Wall quote.

3. Anthony Crupi, What You Need to Know About U.S. Sports TV Contracts, *Sportico,* February 1, 2024.

4. Owen - Quote from Roberts, p. 208.

5. Stephen Fox, *The Mirror Makers: A History of American Advertising and Its Creators*, Vintage Books, 1985.

6. John Carpenter, Augusta National lays out guidelines around Map & Flag hospitality venue, *Sports Business Journal*, March 29, 2024. – Lanyard quote.

7. Jef I. Richards, *A History of Advertising*, Rowman & Littlefield, 2024.

8. Nick Paumgarten, Mr. Money Mustache, the Frugal Guru, *New Yorker*, February 21, 2016. – Peter Adeney

9. Alex Weprin, Charles Barkley Rips Into NBA Over New TV Rights Deals, *Hollywood Reporter*, July 26, 2024.

10. Thomas Bonk, Golf : Are Today's High-Paying Pro Tournaments a Threat to the Masters?, *Los Angeles Times*, April 10, 1988. – Hardin quote.

11. Rick Reilly, Masterful, *Sports Illustrated*, April 18, 1988. – Hardin Pizza Hut quote.

## Chapter Ten

1. Pamela N. Danzinger, Why Zara Succeeds, *Forbes*, April 18, 2018.

2. The marketing and advertising strategy of Zara, *SwiftERM.com*, April 7, 2021.

3. Zeynep Ton, Lessons from Costco on Sustainable Growth, *Harvard Business Review*, March 2024.

4. Hannah Beach, The Real Reason Costco Doesn't Advertise, *Mashed.com*, April 10, 2022.

5. Stephen Greenhouse, How Costco Became the Anti-Walmart, *New York Times*, July 17, 2005. – Sinegal quote.

6. Snyder, p. xxii.

## Chapter Eleven

1. No byline, 2019 Masters Tournament Committee Assignments, *Augusta Chronicle*, April 6, 2019. (Last publicly available committee assignments). Age calculations adjusted to 2024.

2. IBM.com/sports/masters, IBM at the Masters, undated.
3. Samuel Mailer, The Masters 2024 - Innovation and Technology Enhancing 'a Tradition Unlike Any Other', *Marks & Clerk*, April 9, 2024.
4. Alexandra Koch, Check out some of the high-dollar Masters merch hauls that went viral on TikTok, *Augusta Chronicle*, April 17, 2024. – Quote from Marks.
5. David Rumsey, The Masters' Broadcasters Take What They Can Get, *Front Office Sports*, April 10, 2024.- Quote from Noah Syken.
6. Kendall Baker, How the Masters developed the best app in sports, *Axios*, April 13, 2013.
7. Garry Evans, The Weinberg Interview, *Euromoney*, June 1, 1990.
8. Andrew Tolve, Below the Hole: The Masters' underground technology fetish, *Slate*, April 4, 2007. – SubAir.
9. Associated Press, Johnson Stepping Down at Augusta, *Gainesville Sun*, May 6, 2006. – Young quote.
10. No byline, Masters Webcast will Showcase Amen Corner, *ESPN.com*, May 30, 2006. – Johnson quote.
11. Ward Clayton, IBM and Masters.com Celebrate Twenty Years, *Masters.com*, April 2, 2016. – Payne quote.
12. Roberts, p. 222.
13. Chairman Ridley's 2024 Press Conference, *Masters.com*, April 10, 2024.


Chapter Twelve


1. Kat Zeman, Uline, *Supply Chain World Magazine*, May 8, 2019.
2. No byline, *Ikea.com*, July 5, 2022.
3. @Ginnirometty, *Instagram*, April 7, 2023.


Chapter Thirteen


1. Dean M. Schroeder and Alan G. Robinson, America's Most Successful Export to Japan: Continuous Improvement Programs, *Sloan Management Review, MIT*, Spring 1991. – Details on the shipbuilder and shogun.
2. Roberts, p. 55.
3. Price, p. 6.
4. Ron Whitten Illustrations by Chris O'Riley, A Comprehensive History of Every Change Made to Augusta National Golf Club, *Golf Digest*, April 4, 2024.
5. Nick Paumgarten, Inside the Cultish Dreamworld of Augusta National, *New Yorker*, June 14, 2019. – "Oz within Oz" reference.
6. Jack Welch, *Winning*, Harper Business, 2005.

Chapter Fourteen

1.   Jim Garamone, Hicks Make Case that Effective Defense Innovation is Moving Forward, *DOD News*, Jan 30, 2024.
2.   MARADMINS, USMC Continuous Process Improvement (CPI) Implementation Policy, January 7, 2008.
3.   Robert Borries, U.S.A.F. Uses Continuous Process Improvement on the B-2 Bomber: Part 1, February 27, 2024.
4.   U.S. Department of Defense, Continuous Process Improvement Transformation Guidebook, May 2006.
5.   No byline, American Public Television, Steve Jobs and Japan, *aptonline.org*.
6.   Joel M. Podolny and Morten T. Hansen, How Apple is Organized for Innovation, *Harvard Business Review*, November-December 2020.
7.   Adam Lashinsky, *Inside Apple*, Business Plus, 2012. – Quote about packaging, p. 49.
8.   Ben Gilbert and David Rosenthal, "Sony" *Acquired* podcast, March 7, 2022 - Freak quote.
9.   Philip Elmer-Dewitt, Scott Forstall is Apple's 'CEO-in-waiting' says new book, *Fortune*, January 17, 2012.
10.  Ben Cohen. Tim Cook on Why Apple's Huge Bets Will Pay Off, *The Wall Street Journal Magazine*, October, 20, 2024. – Quote about not being first.
11.  Anthony Raymond, *How to set Goals with Kaizen & Ikigai*, 2021.

Chapter Fifteen

1.   Larry Bohannan, Scorecard controversy at 1968 Masters still haunts its champion Bob Goalby, *Desert Sun*, April 1, 2018.
2.   Herbert Warren Wind, Robert Tyre Jones, Jr., *Following Through*, Ticknor & Fields, 1985. p. 138 – Jones quote about respect.
3.   Roberts, p. 220-221.
4.   Kate Murphy, 'Hold Music' Is Annoying. It Doesn't Have to Be That Way, *The Wall Street Journal*, May 21, 2024.
5.   Andrew Ross Sorkin, A Free Market Manifesto That Changed the World, *New York Times*, September 11, 2020.
6.   Milton Friedman, The Social Responsibility of Business is to Increase its Profits, *New York Times Magazine*, September 13, 1970.
7.   A Tough and Inventive Corporate Lawyer, Martin Lipton, W'52, *Wharton Magazine*, July 1, 2007. – Top lawyer reference.
8.   Chris Melore, Supervisor, please, *StudyFinds.org*, September 30, 2022.
9.   *Masters.com* – Davis and Stuckey quotes.
10.  Frank Pingue, Masters patrons a rare breed in wild world of sport, *Reuters.com*, April 11, 2019. – Ridley quote

Chapter Sixteen

1. Mike Troy, Publix Pursues Vision of Service and Ownership, *Progressive Grocer*, November 16, 2020.
2. Jeffrey S. Harrison, Morgan Owdom, Duncan Pitchford, Alex Stratton and Brian Warren, Publix Supermarkets Inc, *Robins School of Business*, University of Richmond, January 2012.
3. Lee Cockerell, *Creating Magic*, Crown Currency, 2008.
4. Walt Disney Company Press Release, Disney Named World's Most Reputable Company, April 15, 2024.
5. Dr. Jeffrey A. Barnes, Pay Attention to the Details, *thewisdomofwalt.com*– Quote from Walt.
6. Joshua Gans, Disney Nailed Attention to Detail Long Before Apple, *Harvard Business Review*, March 26, 2012.- Manhole covers.
7. Joe Pompliano, How Mercedes-Benz Stadium Created a Blueprint For Modern Sports Venues, *Huddle Up*, January 17, 2025. – Best sporting event.
8. @Condoleezza Rice, *Twitter*, November 5, 2024.

Chapter Seventeen

1. Spectator Suggestions for the Masters Tournament – Jones quote.
2. David Coggins, Manners at the Masters, *Masters.com*, April 13, 2019.
3. Mprince, forums.golfwrx.com/topic/1946388-watched-liv-golf-for-the-first-time/, July 3, 2023.
4. Jordan Tidwell, Golf, But Louder : A Look at the Music at LIV Golf, *News 9 Tulsa*, May 10, 2023.
5. No byline, *KHits 106.9 Tulsa*. – Quote from Dolan
6. John Hawkins, LIV May Be 'Golf But Louder' But the Best Watching Experience Was on Mute, *Sports Illustrated*, February 27, 2023.
7. Charlie Roscoe, Noise can harm your health—even if you sleep through it, Harvard T.H. Chan School of Public Health, December 4, 2023.
8. Welcome to the Masters, *ESPN.com*, April 12, 2024. – Fitzpatrick quote.
9. Don Riddell, Inside the Masters bubble, *CNN.com*, April 16, 2024. – Quotes from Augusta chairmen.
10. Steve Keating, Golf: Winds of change will never blow away Augusta tradition, *Reuters*, April 10, 2019. – Ridley quote.
11. Sampson, page xi. – Annual report quote.
12. Price, p. 57.
13. Pete Coors, Cornell University Durland Memorial Lecture, April 18, 2017.

## Chapter Eighteen

1. Joseph McCormack, *Quiet Works*, Matt Holt Books, 2024.
2. Natalie Engels and Sean Gallivan, Adobe's Founders Tower Provides a Glimpse Into the Future of Work, *Gensler.com*, April 12, 2023.
3. Pixar: Incredible Culture Corporate Presentation, accessed at https://www.slideshare.net/slideshow/42910756
4. Legendary Coach Lou Holtz, Golf, Politics, and Life Lessons, *Golf Politics* podcast, July 3, 2024.

## Chapter Nineteen

1. Details of Spencer's ordeal from Owen, pp. 225-226.
2. Associated Press, Q&A with Augusta chairman Hootie Johnson, published on *ESPN.com,* November 11, 2002.
3. Details about the Masters and individual members charitable giving from causeiq.com, Form 990s.
4. Masters Tournament Foundation, *Masters.com.*
5. PGA Tour website, article about charitable giving, December 12, 2023.
6. Sampson, p. 236.
7. Payne quote from *Masters.com.*
8. Matthew Cooper, U.K. broadcasting rights deal, *Daily Mirror*, February 17, 2023.
9. Scott Michaux, Taking a Stand will be Legacy of Johnson, *Augusta Chronicle*, July 15, 2017.
10. Joe Pompliano, The (Secret) Process to Becoming a Member at Augusta National Golf Club, *Huddle Up*, November 8, 2024. – reference to being organized as a for-profit.
11. Herbert Warren Wind, The Call of the Masters, *New Yorker*, April 20, 1962.

## Chapter Twenty

1. Steen Thomsen, Foundation Ownership at Novo Nordisk, *Copenhagen Business School*, May 4, 2016.
2. Matthew Kelly, *The Generosity Habit*, Blue Sparrow, April 2022.
3. John Steinbreder, The Legacy of Tom Cousins, *Global Golf Post*, April 10, 2020. – Nunn quote

## Chapter Twenty-One

1. Tom Wall, Ouimet, Hagen to Tee Off at 1, *Augusta Chronicle*, April 3, 1941. – Grand old men reference.

2.    E. Michael Johnson, The history of Masters honorary starters—from Jock Hutchison to Tom Watson, *Golf Digest*, undated.

3.    John Steinbreder, Elder Makes History Again, *Masters.com*, April 8, 2021. – Elder quotes.

4.    No byline, Augusta National Royalty, *Augusta Magazine*, April 1, 2016.

5.    Staff Writer, Philetus Sawyer Harison, *Augusta Chronicle*, April 30, 2008. – Harison's role.

6.    Owen, quote about relationships, p. 194.

7.    Sam Farmer, Where are the Masters green jackets stored? Exclusive vault opened for first time, *The Los Angeles Times*, April 7, 2023.

8.    No byline, D-Day? What's That?, *The Roper Center for Public Opinion Research*, June 6, 2014.

9.    Marty Smith, *The Masters: Fore Please! Now Driving*...podcast, April 4, 2019. – Reference from O'Laughlin.

Chapter Twenty-Two

1.    Grace Minassian, Why Wimbledon Leaves $60 Million On Centre Court, *Forbes*, August 6, 2018.

2.    Andy Martin, Sally Bolton on planning Wimbledon: 'It's all about attention to detail', *The Independent*, June 22, 2019. – Quote about improving.

3.    Oliver Brown, Sir Ronnie Hampel, former ICI chairman, has played a pivotal role in bringing sport's most prestigious clubs closer together, *Daily Telegraph*, October 23, 2023.

4.    Jon Haworth, 'Christmas in July': Wimbledon's evolution as a lifestyle brand proves it's not just a tennis tournament, *ABC News*, July 3, 2024. – Ashmore quote.

5.    No byline, In Pursuit of Greatness, *Chadwarner.com*, undated. – Quote about grace.

6.    No byline, 30 Best Roger Goodell Quotes With Image, *bookey.com*.

Chapter Twenty-Three

1.    Kyle Porter, Masters 2018 Stunning New Merchandise Shop Part of Bigger Improvements, *cbsports.com*, April 2, 2018.

2.    Minassian, Wimbledon source.

3.    Teitelbaum - revenue estimate for badges, merchandise, and TV.

4.    Sampson, p. xxiv.

5.    Dave Feschuk, The magic of the Masters gnome, *Toronto Star*, April 8, 2023.

6.    Tyler Lauletta, Take a tour of Augusta National's gorgeous pro shop, the only place where you can buy official Masters merchandise, *Business Insider*, April 6, 2023.

7.  Rob Jerram, The Masters 2024: I step inside the purpose-built Augusta shop that takes $1m every hour, *Today's Golfer*, April 11, 2024. – price references

8.  Jimmy Roberts, Take a Look Inside the Main Golf Shop, *Masters.com*, April 2, 2018.

9.  Etan Vlessing, Disney's $56.2B in Retail Sales Leads Global Brand Licensing Race, *The Hollywood Reporter*, July 7, 2022.

10. LinkedIn, Graphic designer job posting, https://lnkd.in/eaefRdFQ, July 29, 2024.

11. Ted Johnson, The Masters: 10 Things They Don't Tell You About Augusta National on TV, *Bleacher Report*, April 4, 2011 – Estimate on attendance figures.

12. Marty Smith, *The Masters: Fore Please! Now Driving...*podcast, April 4, 2021. – Sankey Quote

Chapter Twenty-Four

1.  Kurt Philip, Scarcity Marketing Tactics used by the World's Biggest Brands, *Convertica.com*, undated.

2.  Ben Gilbert and David Rosenthal, "Hermès" *Acquired* podcast, February 19, 2024.

3.  No byline, Everything You Need to Know About Buying an Hermès Bag, *British Vogue*, February 9, 2024.

4.  T. Boone Pickens, *The First Billion is the Hardest*, Crown Currency, 2009.

Chapter Twenty-Five

1.  Bonk – Quote about smoke

2.  No byline, World Golf Hall of Fame Induction Ceremony, June 10, 2019, *ASAP Sports* – Payne quote

3.  Bill Pennington, For a Few Days at Augusta National, the Spotlight Shines on the Women, *New York Times*, April 3, 2022. – Silverstein quote.

Chapter Twenty-Six

1.  @14bisa, in reply to a post on @masters, *Instagram*, April 13, 2024. – quote about father.

2.  Marty Smith, *The Masters: Fore Please! Now Driving...* podcast, April 4, 2019. – Quote from Nantz.

3.  Marty Smith, The Masters: Fore Please! Now Driving...podcast, Episode 3, 2025. – Claire Rogers reference.

4.  Geoff Shackelford, *The Quadrilateral*, April 16, 2024.

5.  Charles Price, *Golfer-At-Large : New Slants on an Ancient Game*, Atheneum, 1982. p. 33

# About the Author

John Sabino is a world-renowned golf blogger and the author of two previous golf books. He is among a small group of golfers who have played the top one hundred ranked golf courses in the world, culminating with Augusta National. John chronicled his journey around the world to complete his quest in a blog that has over 2 million readers. He has written for *Links Magazine* and *Golf Digest* and has been featured in *Australian Golf Digest*, *The Star Ledger*, *Links Magazine*, *The Wall Street Journal*, *Golf Digest Index*, *Luxury Travel Magazine*, *Il Mondo del Golf Today (Italian Golf Digest)*, *Perfect Eagle Golf Magazine* (Germany) and *Billionaire Magazine*.

John is a retired financial services executive and spent more than thirty-five years working for various firms in New York City. He splits his time between the golf-rich state of New Jersey—home to the number one ranked golf course in the world and the USGA—and Bluffton, South Carolina, a two-and-a-half-hour drive from Augusta National via the Augusta Highway.

John is a cancer survivor and is seven years out from his bone marrow transplant to treat leukemia. He survived through the grace of God, the loving support of his family and friends, and the amazing team that treats him at the Hospital of the University of Pennsylvania.